KU-825-414

FULL
CIRCLE

FULL
CIRCLE

JANE HERSEY

Copyright © 2013 Jane Hersey

The moral right of the author has been asserted.

Apart from any fair dealing for the purposes of research or private study,
or criticism or review, as permitted under the Copyright, Designs and Patents
Act 1988, this publication may only be reproduced, stored or transmitted, in
any form or by any means, with the prior permission in writing of the
publishers, or in the case of reprographic reproduction in accordance with
the terms of licences issued by the Copyright Licensing Agency. Enquiries
concerning reproduction outside those terms should be sent to the publishers.

Matador
9 Priory Business Park
Kibworth Beauchamp
Leicestershire LE8 0RX, UK
Tel: (+44) 116 279 2299
Fax: (+44) 116 279 2277
Email: books@troubador.co.uk
Web: www.troubador.co.uk/matador

ISBN 978 1780884 295

British Library Cataloguing in Publication Data.
A catalogue record for this book is available from the British Library.

Typeset in 11.5pt Minion Pro by Troubador Publishing Ltd, Leicester, UK
Printed and bound in the UK by TJ International, Padstow, Cornwall

Matador is an imprint of Troubador Publishing Ltd

MIX
Paper from
responsible sources
FSC
www.fsc.org   FSC® C013056

Dedicated to my son Paul

FOREWORD

In my review of Jane Hersey's dark, dense and disturbing first book *Breath In The Dark*, I mentioned how writing about childhood can sometimes be a disconsolate, if not solipsistic undertaking – even if just from the premise of trying to remember. Writing about a traumatic childhood can be tougher still, even if just from the standpoint of deciding what to leave out and what to include. Whereas writing about a childhood that is fraught with the regularity of haunting darkness and abuse, might, in some instances, be deemed almost impossible; even if just from the presupposition of either wanting to move on or simply forget.

In Hersey's case, the fruition of her invaluable darkness has ultimately enabled her to see a far bigger, brighter light, than most.

Apart from providing the authoress with an admittedly untoward foundation, her initial foreboding ensured that a rather sagacious sense of understanding and considered reasoning would forever prevail. Indeed, it set the parameters, by which she conducted her alarmingly distressing teenage years, which, as is evident throughout *Full Circle*, evolved into a life more poetically prone to the needs and susceptibility of others. And in this day and (unfortunate) age of Styrofoam compassion and designer poverty, there really aren't a lot of people one can say that about.

On the one hand, this could be viewed as woefully meritorious, while on the other, construed as a crystal clear continuation of inner-self-loathing.

Having worked in Social Services for a number of years, I have to say it is normally the latter that rears its harrowingly complex head on an all too regular, self-destructive, basis. Without a readily acknowledged discerning outlet or network of support - let alone living, loving parents – the usual port of call with regards child abuse, is the ill-conceived, introspective, self. So when Hersey writes: "I lowered my head at the mention of my name, I knocked on the doctor's door," or: "I looked in the mirror. I still had food in my mouth. My heart was pounding and I felt weak, "I hate you." I whispered repeatedly. I opened my coat and pulled my trousers down to my knees. Hitting myself between my legs with my shoe, I knew I had to get all the food out of my stomach [...]," it doesn't come as a complete and utter shock to the system.

Unsettling images both, they nevertheless portray a young girl's way of dealing with a seemingly impossible situation that was absolutely not of her own design. Yet, what makes the above all the more shocking, if such be the word, is the fact that not only has the writer had the courage to recollect, reflect upon and admit said words; she's also felt the compunctious need to write them down and chronologically place them somewhere in a book.

***

As much a book of agonising sincerity as it is inadvertent, inner-strength; *Full Circle* is, if nothing else, a book of hope.

Like the Tim Robbins character in *The Shawshank*

Redemption, the older Jane Hersey throughout these pages, subliminally assists those who are willing, able and consenting enough, to find their own fortitude. Their our own truth. Regardless of familial anguish, tortuous ridicule, dismissive negligence, sexual exploitation and dare I write, unspeakable violence: "My face shot from side to side with the force of his fists punching me [...]. I noticed the pattern on the sole of his boot as he kicked my face [...]. The pain was unbearable. I picked myself off the floor, deciding to sleep on the floor in the baby's room."

Such lack of self-regard as having to "sleep on the floor" of her own "baby's room," is further exasperated when placed alongside the rampant anti-Semitism of Jane's early years. Was it not for the fact that as a young Jewish girl, she might not have known any better (which was probably just as well), the endemically racist quagmire in which the teenager found herself, could, from that of her ancestral perspective at least, have been so much worse. Although surely not a whole lot more in relatively modern day Britain: "I've seen the Angel of Death upstairs. It's because she's a Jew. We'll have to move from here [...]. Don't stand near to her."

To think these words were spoken in 1970s Liverpool rather than 1930s Munich, really does take some getting used to. But then so do a number of despicable things in life.

That the authoress has had the courage to share just some of her woebegone youth is clearly commendable. That she has done so by way of unfolding the folded lie of societal expectation and its unnecessarily ingrained hypocrisy - much of which is due to the current day media's knee-jerk reaction towards racism and its sensationalist reportage of sexual child abuse - is furthermore, audacious, not to mention critical. As the writer and Lecturer in Law and Criminology at Ulster University, Anne-Marie McAlinden has written in her recently published, excellent second book *'Grooming' and the Sexual Abuse of Children* (Oxford University Press - 2012) "Until we have an effective child protection statutory system plus an effective public education awareness programme, things won't change."

Were it not for the tragedy of innocence that underlines *Full Circle* with more tenderness than ought to be allowed, words such as frank and focused, dense and delicate, humble and heartbreaking, would surely be deemed redundant. As is, Jane Hersey has herein written an unforgettably, powerful book - poignantly dedicated to her son Paul.

In fact, what's written amid these pages is a crucial execution of the most suave and sensitive persuasion. At times so harrowing it nigh borders on a comedic precipice of the quasi-absurd, the circularity of its ethos is (almost) enough to make one break down and cry. Not so much because of the crime-ridden cruelty and idiosyncratic ignorance; but rather, the writer's inexorable and unquestionable belief in the potentiality for human kindness and humility.

Perhaps love, is the word I'm looking for?

David Marx
St. Girons, France
January 2013

PREFACE

I was now 16 years old and remained traumatised and haunted by my past; I over-trusted people and had an overriding urge to protect them and prevent them from feeling any emotional pain. I was psychologically living on the edge of society and was socially isolated. I had not developed the mindset to question this. Looking back it was in reality an enforced imprisonment, meaning I did not have the emotional, educational, financial means or support to change my predicament.

As I grew into womanhood my confusion at the world became more apparent. I was taking comfort in behaviours that were familiar, not bathing, wearing multiple layers of clothes and, like my mother, I was bingeing on food. Of course I was still very much a lonely unsupported child myself when I got pregnant – one who had never been nurtured or mothered and as such I struggled with the responsibilities of parenthood.

Marginalised and abused children are often overlooked even today, and risk becoming marginalised and abused adults who may never receive acknowledgement or respect for the immense physical and emotional burden they carry from childhood, or indeed have their full potential realised.

CHAPTER 1

Windermere 1970

"My name's Jane Levene." I told the receptionist, my head slightly bowed. Looking around the large reception area, there were no Jewish faces. I wondered if anyone knew my name was really Hikey. I watched as she used a ruler to draw a line in a very large ledger.

"I feel like I've been here forever and a day," she said, without lifting her head. She seemed kindly, small, slender and frail, like Beverly's mother. Another woman appeared.

"I'm the housekeeper." She beckoned me towards a long corridor. I followed her up a small flight of stairs to a smaller corridor. "This is your room, we're expecting more staff. For the moment you have the room to yourself." I looked out of the window. The drive was tree lined. "The back lawn leads onto Lake Windermere. I'll leave you to unpack."

"Thank you." The room was bare except for a bunk bed in the corner and a small chest of drawers beside it. I pushed my suitcase under the bed. "This is your new home, Hikey." I put my arms around myself.

The housekeeper returned. "We're short staffed at the moment, you'll have to wait on at dinner, be in the kitchen for seven o'clock, silver service. Do you have a black skirt and white blouse?"

"No."

"Well get them! Borrow them." She left the room. I opened the door slightly in case of fire and switched the light on and off three times. I sat beside the bundle of bedding she had left for me. Holding my tummy, I could smell the countryside, desperately wanting to run home. I watched the door, half expecting Mrs Lichenstein or Matron to walk in with a glass of egg and milk. The door opened. I held my hand to my nose, covering my profile.

"What's your name?" A young woman asked.

"Jane Levene." I mumbled frowning.

"I'm Julie. I'm a chambermaid. What's the matter with your face?"

"Nothing," I replied, my head bowed.

"Are you coming outside to sunbathe?"

"No, I'm tired. I'm having a *shloff.*" I said, wishing she would go away.

"A what?"

"Nothing," I whispered, opening my suitcase. Packed on top of the clothes were three Mars bars and three packets of crisps. I pushed them under the pillow. Reaching for the blanket that was neatly folded at the foot of the bed and wrapping myself in it, I curled up, comforted by the warmth. "*Gehen shloffen*, Hikey."

I awoke, my heart banging so loudly and rapidly I thought it would explode. Feeling my pulse, gasping to get the air to the bottom of my lungs, my heart had stopped. I stood up, stamping my foot hard on the floor. I felt my pulse again, this time I could feel my heart beating. Laying down on the bed once more and relieved to be alive, I was shaking uncontrollably. Feeling very hungry I ripped the paper off the Mars bars eating them in quick succession. Soon all the crisps had been eaten as well. I could hear voices outside the bedroom. The door opened again.

"It's our teatime," a young woman with black curly hair said in a broad Liverpool accent. "I'm Anne. Come on, I'll show you where the kitchen is. My friend Babs is down there. Are you waiting on later?"

"Yes."

"Have you done silver service before?"

"No, I was nearly a punch card operator. I can make backs and sleeves."

We joined the queue in the kitchen. The chef handed each person a plate of cold meat and salad. My heart sank. I knew that would never fill me up. "I'm very hungry." He looked at me and placed some boiled new potatoes on my plate. "Thank you." I followed the girls to the staff room. Sitting on an easy chair, in the corner of the room, my head bowed, I devoured all the food on the plate. For a moment I watched the young people sat around the table. I didn't want to sit with them. One of the girls caught my eye. I looked away, covering my nose. I heard giggling. The housekeeper appeared.

"Come on girls, it's time for service." We followed her to the main kitchen where the chef was preparing the evening meals. "I told you to borrow a black skirt and white blouse. You'd better take your coat off." The other girls went through to the dining room to take orders. Soon all the orders were piling up, everyone was rushing about the kitchen. The housekeeper handed me a silver platter along with a large spoon and fork. On the platter were four grilled plaice. "I told you to take off your coat!"

"I want to be a chambermaid. I don't know how to do this." She pointed me in the direction of the dining room doors.

"Table nine. Go on!" I pushed the door open using my back.

"There are people out there." I said my hands shaking.

"They're waiting for their meals. Go on." I was in the dining room. My legs froze as I watched all the people eating. I looked for the kitchen door pushing my way back through it. The housekeeper looked at me, then at the platter containing the plaice.

"I don't like it out there." I turned around and the plaice landed on the floor.

"Can I work in the bedrooms please?"

"Yes!" She snapped. I went back to the bedroom hoping I wouldn't get the sack. Sitting on the bed with my suitcase on my lap, I held it tightly, it felt so warm and comforting. I wondered how long I would be able to stay here. Opening the case I looked at my photographs and candlesticks. The housekeeper entered the room. "Report to the kitchen at six thirty a.m, and you can have your breakfast. You're on morning teas before you start the rooms."

"What's morning teas?"

"It's for people who want tea in their rooms before breakfast."

"OK," I felt very tired and hungry. The hotel was miles from the nearest shop. I decided to cover myself with the blankets and sleep. Later in the evening Julie knocked on the bedroom door. "We're going out for a drink. Do you want to come with?"

"No thank you."

"What do you drink when you go out? We all drink Cherry B and cider."

"I had kosher wine at Auntie Doris's. The room spun around."

They left the room giggling. I knew they were only pretending to know what they were doing. I remembered the large fridges in the kitchen downstairs. Perhaps there was some leftovers. I walked down the corridor, into the kitchen. I noticed a slab of fruitcake cut into slices. I ate one slice putting two more in my pocket. The large fridge was padlocked. The smaller fridge had some cheese wrapped in foil and quickly, I grabbed it. The darkness lifted in anticipation of eating. I went into the staff room, switched on the television and sat in the easy chair. I had heard someone say that the television was a useful tool for learning. The news was on. Each word I heard beginning with 'E' I practised, hoping no member of staff was called Eric. The door opened. I covered my nose.

"What's your name?"

"Jane Levene," I replied. She smiled. Perhaps she needed me I thought, I wasn't sure. I smiled at her not knowing if it was the right thing to do. "I'm not English, I'm British." I blurted. She looked at me. Immediately I knew I should have kept my big mouth shut.

"Can I change channels?" she asked.

"Yes, I'm going to *shloff*."

"What?"

"To sleep, I'm very tired." I got into bed, curled up and slept. I woke up, expecting the Matron from the Sarah Laski Home to walk in or staff from Delamere to pass me on the stairs. My head felt heavy.

The morning arrived. I was on morning teas. I went down to the kitchen and joined the queue. There was toast, bacon, sausages and eggs. I piled my plate high. The staff were sitting around the table. I sat in the corner on the easy chair. My food secure on my lap I looked for a moment then remembered my nose wasn't covered. I moved to one side so they couldn't see my face. Eating quickly I realised my intestines were blocked. I ran to the nearest toilet managing to get most of the food out of my tummy. It didn't feel full any more it felt cold and empty. I went back to the kitchen and looked for more food. The housekeeper called me as I walked down the corridor and I followed her into a small room. There were shelves stacked with cups and saucers, milk jugs and different size teapots.

"Take your coat off."

"I can't. I'm cold."

"You can't do morning teas with your coat on." All the old feelings filled my head, I felt faint, cold and hungry. I wanted to lie down and sleep. I unbuttoned my coat and put it over the chair. Looking at my list, I knocked on the first room.

"Morning tea."

"Come in." I heard a man's voice. My body tensed. How could I stop myself smelling his body? The room was dark as I pushed the door open holding my breath. My eyes half closed so I wouldn't see him. I put the tray down and rushed from the room. After morning teas were finished the housekeeper walked over to me, dropping a bundle of laundry and a list of room numbers at my feet.

"Collect your cleaning materials from the room next door."

Feeling tired, desperate, cold and empty, I pushed the door open. A terrible smell of socks and bodies greeted me. I knew a man was staying in this room. Looking at the next room number, I opened the door. I could smell perfume. Women's clothes were on the bed. I lay down and slept.

"Miss Levene!" The housekeeper was shouting. She pushed the door open. "What the *hell* are you doing?"

"Having a *shloff*."

"Get off that bed. You are here to work not sleep." I could see her lips moving, she was waving her hands. I was back at Auntie Doris's. "You're going to have to finish the room quickly. You're running behind time. You'll miss lunch if you carry on like this."

Three o'clock arrived and all the staff rushed to their rooms to change into their swimming costumes. The housekeeper was checking all the rooms. She shouted me. "This bathroom floor hasn't been cleaned properly, the tiles are dirty. Here's a list of things you need to go over." After I had finished I went to my room and sank into my bed. It was the only place I wanted to be.

"Are you coming outside, on the back lawn?"

"I need to *shloff*. I'm tired."

Feeling very hungry, I dragged myself out of bed and headed for the kitchen, praying I would find some food. Others were picking at the cake, looking in the fridge. I took some bread and cheese and went back to bed. The door creaked open. I covered the side of my face with my hand. Four female staff were watching me. I kept on eating.

"We're Geordies."

"I'm *fechalished*. I'm very hungry."

"What! Are *you* Jewish?" One of the women asked.

"No."

I was getting very homesick for Manchester. On my day off I decided to visit Auntie Doris. I arrived in Manchester. Auntie Doris's front door was in sight. Reaching for the letter box, I knocked on the door. Hearing footsteps, my heart was thumping, I stamped my foot on the step to keep me alive. I froze as the door opened and slowly smiled.

"Hello, Auntie Doris."

"What do you want?" She frowned.

"Nothing," I bowed my head.

"Well that's good because I'm busy." The door closed. I waited a few moments then walked back towards the bus stop.

CHAPTER 2

It was late when I arrived back at the hotel. The place was in darkness except for a few night lights. My heart racing, I sniffed to make sure there was no burning smoke in the air. I rushed to the staff quarters staying close to the wall, petrified of the dark. As I approached the staff room I could hear voices, the door was open. One of the chambermaids walked in.

"You'll never guess what's happened? The girls from Liverpool, Anne and Babs, have left. They've taken most of the cutlery and a lot of other things."

"I like Anne and Babs." I said my head lowered.

"That's not all. The chef's gone as well, with most of the food. The manager said the guests will have to eat breakfast in groups of four, till we get more stuff. They've taken some of your things."

My suitcase was under the bed. I pulled it out. My photographs were lying in the bottom with two Mars bars, a bra and the candlesticks. They had taken the black midi coat and trousers, all I had left were the clothes I was wearing. Feeling very sad they had gone I got into bed and soon fell asleep.

"Jane, Jane." I was woken by Julie.

"There's a phone call for you."

"Perhaps it's Auntie Doris?"

"No, Anne's on the phone. They're in Bowness. They want to speak to you." I rushed to the telephone. I hoped they hadn't come to any harm.

"Jane, is that you?"

"Yes, Anne. Are you OK?"

"Look, Jane. We've got a lot of stuff here from the hotel. Your trousers are a bit big. We need a suitcase so we can go home. Can we have yours?"

"Yes. What should I do?" I couldn't bear the thought of them not being able to get back home.

"Order a taxi and ask them to bring the suitcase to Bowness. We'll meet it outside the Stags Head Hotel. Don't forget to pay for the taxi, will you?"

"No, Anne." I put the receiver down and looked for the phone number, quickly I ordered the taxi. "Please hurry. Anne and Babs have to get home." I waited near the side door, holding the suitcase. The taxi arrived and I handed it to the driver, along with the money to cover the fare. "Please hurry, they need it straight away." I went back to my bedroom and slept.

The following morning I was woken by a knock on the door, it was my wake up call. I rushed to the kitchen and begged for as much food as possible. The housekeeper followed me and watched for a while. "You must sort yourself out, clean yourself up. Take off your coat. I can't go on warning you. Some of the girls have complained you're disturbing them at night. You wake up shouting."

Why was she telling me these things? What had I done wrong? When I had finished my work I went to the kitchen and found some food. There was some cake in one of the bins. I grabbed it and went upstairs to the staff toilet. I sat on the floor my throat thirsty for food, stuffing myself with all the cake. It needed to go down as quickly as possible. My head felt so heavy and numb it was difficult to get off the floor. I stood over the toilet and put my finger down my throat. The food didn't come back. I needed to be rid of it or nobody would love me. I noticed a bar of soap and rubbed my finger on it making sure some was stuck under my nail. I rammed it down my throat till my stomach started to empty. I looked in the mirror, my face looked bloated and red. My eyes and nose were streaming liquid. I could see my mother. I was desperately tired. I sat on the floor feeling too weak to get up. Someone was banging on the door. I opened it. It was one of the waitresses. I was so desperate to sleep I went to bed and wrapped my arms around myself.

"Wake up!"

My eyes were still closed. I wasn't sure whether I was dreaming or not. My body was shaking I opened my eyes. A young man was lying beside me on the bed.

"I'm Bill. I think you're really beautiful." I remained silent. "Please. I want to make love to you, tonight."

"I need to *shloff*. I'm tired."

"I'll come back at midnight," he insisted.

"No, I need to *shloff*. Please go away." I wondered if he had any family. He might be lonely.

The door creaked. I heard giggling. Looking towards the door several of the staff were there watching. Bill jumped off the bed.

"You don't know what you're missing." He smiled, revealing his one tooth.

My heart felt heavy. I shouldn't have sent him away. Maybe he needed me? Perhaps he didn't have a sister anymore? The thoughts kept repeating in my head over and over. I'll never be able to forgive myself for hurting him. My head was aching. I couldn't sleep.

In the morning it was difficult to find the energy to get out of bed. I knew I had to do my work. I had to please the housekeeper. I felt very ill. I could hardly speak, my throat was so sore. Sleeping on and off in the rooms I was cleaning, finding it too hard to stay awake. I ate all the left over biscuits on the tea trays.

"Is it dinner time?" I asked one of the staff.

"Five minutes." How could I last that long? My stomach ached badly. The kitchen was bursting with staff. There were plenty of new faces. I piled my plate with food, looking to see how much everyone else had on their plates, and hurried to the staff room so I could sit on the chair in the corner, hiding my nose from everyone. I wanted to do the washing up so I could have the leftovers. The others sat around the table. One of the waitresses came over.

"Why did you give Anne and Babs your suitcase? They *stole* your things."

"They needed it to get home."

"I can't believe what I'm hearing. By giving them your case, you helped them steal all that stuff." I could hear giggling.

All the things that Auntie Doris had said to me were reeling in my head. They wouldn't go away. I needed to eat more. I waited near the laundry room with the other chambermaids to get paid. Julie tapped me on the shoulder.

"Come on, we're all going into Bowness, come with us." She smiled.

"I'm very tired." I started walking towards the bedroom, she followed me.

"Look, it's nice and sunny outside. We're going to buy some new clothes. You need some. You can't wear that black gear in this weather. We won't take no for an answer." She stopped in front of me.

"OK." My heart sank. I didn't like the sun. It filled my head with sadness, preferring to be in bed in the dark. We waited outside the hotel for the other girls, then walked into Bowness.

"You've put on a lot of weight since you've been here. I think you'd look good in a pair of hot-pants." She walked off and I heard faint laughter. I was relieved when we reached the shops. I kept feeling my pulse, making sure my lungs had enough air in them to keep me alive.

"Here's the boutique. Jane, don't dawdle!"

I watched as they looked through the rails of clothing, they all seemed very excited. I noticed one of the girls rummaging through a basket with different items of clothing in it.

"Here. Look what I've found." She dashed towards me.

"These should fit you." She was holding a large pair of maroon velvet hot-pants, a cropped jumper and a tank top. "Come on. You try the hot-pants, I'll try the jumper."

"No."

"They'll look great on you." She pulled me towards the changing room. I put them on and opened the curtain. "You look fabulous. She'll take them." The clothes I had been wearing were put in a bag. I paid for the three items, as we left the shop I put my coat back on.

"Let's go for some tea and cake. Take your coat off, it's nice and warm." Julie said.

"No. I don't want to."

"Jane, order cakes and tea for six. You pay, we'll divi up later," one of them said.

"When are we going back to the hotel?" I asked. There was no answer. After we had eaten we went outside.

"That's a good area to sunbathe. Take your coat off."

I watched as they lay back on the grass, soaking up the sun. I found a dark corner and curled up. "Please don't wake me I need to *shloff*." My head rested on the bag with my trousers in it, my eyes closed.

"We'll hang around till the pubs open."

"Time to go. Jane what do you drink?"

"Lemonade."

"No, I mean beer or something. You must drink wine or beer?"

"I've only ever had kosher wine at Auntie Doris's. I didn't like it."

"How much money have you got?" I pulled my wage packet out of my pocket. The pub was packed, I didn't like the smell. Everybody was smoking.

"Where's your money?" I handed her a ten shilling note.

I was getting very tired. "Please can I have some crisps and peanuts?"

"Here." Stretching over to me, she passed two packets of crisps and two packets of peanuts. She handed me a glass. "That's cider." Then she handed me a small bottle. "That's Cherry B, go on. Drink some of the cider. Then add some Cherry B.

I tried some cider and gagged. She grabbed the bottle off me and started pouring it into my glass. "Go on, drink it." They were all saying. I gulped it down.

"I don't like it." Soon I began to feel light headed, the girl holding the bottle of Cherry B poured more into the glass.

"Don't be soft, drink it. It's your round again."

"Alright. I'll have a bit more." My face was burning up. I couldn't stop laughing.

"Give me some more money. I'll get you another one."

I could see the hotel staff moving to the other side of the pub. I handed her my money and she bought another round of drinks. I was standing as near to the wall as possible.

"Come over here with everyone else. We want to sit down," one of the girls shouted. I looked to see if there was a wall I could stand close to, before making a move. I followed them and found a seat near the wall.

"What are you laughing at?"

"I don't know." I replied. One of the girls sat beside me.

"Are you a Jew?"

"No." I told her, covering my nose.

"What does *shloff* mean?"

"To sleep in Yiddish."

"Is your father a Jew-boy?"

"No."

"Why do Jews get buried standing up?"

"I don't know. I'm British, not English."

"Is *she* for real?"

The next thing I remember was trying hard to walk through the side door of the hotel. I followed everyone else. My legs didn't want to move. My tummy couldn't hold the alcohol. I heaved up all the contents. I was pleased about that.

"Are you coming out tomorrow night?"

"No." I replied, following the others to the kitchen to look for food.

"Here's some cheese and cake," one of the girls shouted. I grabbed some of the food and went to my bedroom. I curled up in bed and wished I could stay there forever.

CHAPTER 3

I sat watching the news on the television, trying hard to speak like the newsreader and cure my stammer. The staff were getting ready to go to the pub. I had a plate full of food on my lap. I couldn't wait to finish so I could go to bed and practice some words before sleeping but the words wouldn't sink in.

"Do you mind if I change the channel?" I looked up. A young man was standing there. This was his first day.

"No," I replied.

"How long have you been here?"

"About a month," I frowned. *You'd better not ask me if I'm Jewish*, I thought to myself. He sat watching the television. I finished my food and put my plate on the table.

"Are you going out with the others?"

"No. I'm going to bed."

"Would you like to listen to some records in my room?"

"No, I need to *shloff.*"

"Sorry?"

"Nothing," I replied. I walked through the kitchen on my way to bed, to see if there was any food lying about. The housekeeper followed me.

"I need to talk to you." I stood close to the wall. "This is your last warning, you must tidy yourself. I checked your bed. You haven't changed your sheets. I noticed blood stains in the bed. If there's no change by next week, you're sacked!" She walked off.

"OK," I whispered.

The housekeeper woke me the following morning. "Don't forget what I told you last night, one more week for me to see an improvement and I think I'm being over generous at that."

The young man was in the staff room, eating his breakfast. "My name's Paul."

I kept my head lowered. Does he need me, I wondered?

"Are you going out tonight?" I lifted my head slightly and looked at him. "I only want to talk to you, I don't like going out drinking, that's all they want to do."

I covered my nose and finished my meal. Perhaps he hasn't got any family. Maybe he hasn't got anyone to care for him. I kept quiet.

"See you later. What sort of music do you like?"

"Soul music. I had a radio at Auntie Doris's."

I finished my day's work and went to the kitchen to find some leftovers. A few slices of cheese and cake would take the cold and hunger away for a while. I walked back to the staff quarters, staying close to the wall. I wanted to cry because I knew how empty that young man felt. He was all alone in the world. Perhaps he needed me.

"Are you coming outside to sunbathe? Go get your hot-pants." I heard giggles.

"No, I'm going to bed."

"Miss Levene." My eyes opened, my heart skipped a beat. It was the housekeeper, standing by my bed. What had I done wrong?

"I'm going to have to ask you to leave, I'm sorry. Your final wage packet will be ready on Friday." She left the room. One of the girls walked in.

"Have you been sacked?"

"Yes."

"Are you going home?"

"No."

Paul knocked on the door. "Someone said you've been sacked?"

"Yes."

"Where will you go?"

"I don't know." He was holding a piece of paper.

"It's the phone number of a hotel in Knutsford, they're looking for staff. I could have had a job there."

He left the room. I closed my eyes and slept. The following morning after breakfast, I rang the hotel in Knutsford. I spoke to the manager. He told me there was a vacancy for a chambermaid to start as soon as possible. I worked the following days, then made my journey to Knutsford. When I arrived I was pleased to see the hotel was smaller than the one I had left. It was very old and much darker inside. I felt more secure and happy. The housekeeper met me at the reception desk. I only had the carrier bag with my photos, and candlesticks in. She took me to the staff quarters and showed me the bedroom I would be sharing with three other girls.

"Have you done morning teas before?"

"Oh yes, I'm good at morning teas."

"Fine, you're on morning tea. Would you like a call in the morning?"

"Yes, please." I sat on the bed for a moment, I cried at the thought of all the people I had left behind who needed me. "This is your new home now, Hikey. Go to *shloff* I love you." Pulling the blankets back, I got into bed and held my breasts tightly. I soon closed my eyes and slept. I awoke in the early hours. The nightmare had woken me. We had passed through the kitchen on the way to the bedroom. I was desperately hungry. Hoping there would be plenty of food I made my way downstairs. I noticed two whole cheeses. I checked them to see if they had been cut into. There was a shelf with plates of uncooked meat. My heart sank. "Please God help me, I need food." Sitting in the corner of the room my eyes closed. The desire to curl up and sleep was too powerful.

"What are you doing?" I opened my eyes slowly, the bright lights hurt them. The manager was standing in front of me. "You shouldn't be in here."

"Sorry," I said. Getting up, I edged away from him, my head bowed. I didn't mean to hurt his feelings. Maybe he needs me to care for him, maybe he doesn't have a family.

"The kitchen's out of bounds at night!" He frowned.

"OK."

The following morning I was woken by the housekeeper. I was on morning teas. I rushed to the kitchen, combing my hair on the way and straightening my trousers. I had made my mind up not to wear the hot pants ever again. I told the chef how hungry I felt. He was a very big man, and spoke in broken English. I wondered if he was Jewish.

"Chips, I don't mess. I only do chips. You like."

"Yes please, lots." I watched as he piled my plate high with chips.

"Please can I have some bread as well?" I begged.

"Get from there, you big girl." I looked but couldn't see the bread. "From there, you stupid." He looked very angry and irritable. His face was getting redder by the minute.

"I don't want chips for my breakfast. Are you bloody mad?" I heard a young man say to the chef.

"You no like. You don't have. You want continental breakfast, maybe. You ask see if you get."

The argument carried on. I went to the staffroom and devoured my chips. The housekeeper handed me two lists, one for morning teas the other for cleaning the bedrooms. Looking at the lists I noticed two rooms wanted breakfast in bed. My head ached, what if they were men? What if I smell their bodies? What if they needed me to care for them? More staff came into the staff room. I covered my nose and stayed silent.

"What's your name?"

"Jane Levene. I'm not Jewish. Honestly." I ran from the staff room. "I'm English not British. No. I'm British not English." I was mumbling, I couldn't remember which way round it was. I kept repeating these things under my breath. First five times to see if I could remember then ten times. Soon my head ached so much I had to sleep in one of the rooms before starting work.

"Miss Levene." I was woken by the sound of the housekeeper's voice. "You've not done any morning teas. This will never do. Hurry, get them done. Now! Get your coat off."

The manager was at the end of the corridor I watched for a moment as they talked. I hoped they weren't going to sack me. Sitting on the bed my head was full of darkness. "Don't worry Hikey I love you." My mind felt darker. "Jane Levene I hate you." I whispered.

I noticed three packets of biscuits on the breakfast tray. The need for food was overwhelming. There was momentary relief till the feelings of isolation, cold and hunger filled my mind once more. I rushed to the toilet and stuck my fingers down my throat. "I hate you." I whispered. My body felt too tired and weak to move. My eyes and nose gushing liquid, I could feel how red and bloated my face had become after vomiting. I lay on the bed, the urge to sleep too desperate. After some time I opened my eyes. My heart banging I rushed out of the bedroom towards the linen room. Two more chambermaids queued behind me.

"The housekeeper should be here in a minute. What happened to that girl's mother?" one asked.

"She had a heart attack, they thought it was indigestion at first, she got a bad pain in her chest and down her arm. She died on the way to hospital."

I listened, wishing the housekeeper would open the door, so I could collect the bed linen. I knew I was behind with my work. We heard her footsteps. She opened the door and I collected what I needed. I carried them along the corridor, placing them outside the bedroom door. Suddenly, my arm felt limp, a terrible pain shot up it and across my chest, I felt breathless and light headed. I knew I was having a heart attack, I was dying. The words of the chambermaid echoed in my head. I fell against the wall. I mustn't die. What if mum, Jeffery and David needed me? I couldn't stop my life from ebbing away, I gasped for air, so I would stay alive. "Please get a doctor, I'm dying." Picking myself off the floor, I ran down the corridor. The housekeeper rushed out of the linen room following me. She looked at me. I felt my pulse. I was barely alive. "Please call a doctor. I'm dying." I was still standing, I wasn't dead. The housekeeper looked at me. I walked back to the bedroom, laid on the bed and fell asleep. My body couldn't carry me. It was impossible to keep my eyes open.

"Miss Levene, Miss Levene." My body was shaking. I opened my eyes. "You're here to work, not sleep!" The housekeeper was very angry.

"Sorry."

"You're on a warning. Get your lunch. Then start work straight away. The other chambermaids are well into their work. You'll have to carry on till you've done yours."

I made my way to the kitchen. The staff were waiting to be served. The chef was dishing out plates of chips.

"We don't want bloody chips," one of the porters shouted.

"I'll have them," I begged the chef. He looked like someone's nice grandfather. I knew he needed me. I didn't want the other staff to shout at him. I wanted to protect him. I knew how kind and loving he was. I ate my large plate of chips and eventually finished my work. I found some food in the kitchen and went back to my room.

"There's a phone call for you."

I walked towards the phone, hoping I wouldn't die on the way, in case it was David. I lifted the receiver.

"It's Paul from the hotel in Bowness."

"Hello."

"What's the hotel like?" He asked.

"OK. I'm very tired. I'm going to bed now."

It was almost teatime. The staff walked past the bedroom on their way to the kitchen. Getting out of bed I rushed in case all the food had been eaten. The kitchen was in uproar. The chef was handing out plates of chips.

"Fucking chips, again. What sort of a fucking chef are you? A fucking chip chef." One of the barman shouted.

"I'm going to get the manager," the porter said. "Fucking chips again. We'll all end up looking like you."

My heart ached. I didn't like them shouting at him, I wanted to care for him. "I'll have the chips." He piled more chips on my plate. "Thank you." I smiled.

The manager dashed past the room and I could hear shouting from the kitchen. I ate my meal and went to bed. In the evening I was so desperate to eat. All the food had been locked in the fridges. There was nothing. I left the hotel and started walking, praying some shops would be open. Maybe a fish and chip shop. I could smell food. The smell was getting stronger. I could feel tears in my eyes. I held my tummy and prayed that I would soon feel some relief from all the pain. I found an entry by the side of the shop and ate my food. My body stopped shaking. I needed more. I heard loud music coming from a pub further down the road, a notice was on the door, *Disco and free meal.* I checked my pockets, finding some loose change. I walked up the steps to the pub and paid my entrance fee.

"Where do I get my free meal?" I was directed to a hatch where I handed my ticket to a young woman. "What's the free meal?"

"Deep fried meat and potato pie with chips."

"Please can I have lots of chips?" She returned holding a paper plate full of food, with a white plastic fork lying on top. "Thank you." I found a seat against the wall, and started eating.

"Would you like to dance?" a young man asked.

"No." He walked away, I lifted my head. "I've hurt him, he needs me. How could I ever forgive myself? I looked around but couldn't see him. I started crying. I finished my meal and went back to the hotel.

In the morning I felt very ill, hot and listless, I could hardly talk. A young woman entered the room and started unpacking her clothes.

"What's it like being a chambermaid here?"

"It's nice."

"Have you got a sore throat? You sound rough."

"It hurts badly. Do you know what time it is?"

"Nine o'clock."

I got out of bed and rushed to the linen room.

"You *must* take your coat off," the housekeeper said.

"No, I can't."

"I'm afraid your work's not up to standard. Do you wear sanitary towels? I found blood covered toilet roll under your bed."

"Have I got the sack?"

"Yes."

"Please can I stay till I get somewhere else to go?" She looked at me.

"Until the end of the week," she turned and left the room.

One of the chambermaids pushed the door open. "The chef's gone he's pinched all the food. Chips for breakfast, lunch and tea, he was bloody mad." I felt very sad.

The following day I was too ill to work. I went to see a doctor. I sat on the seat beside him. I bowed my head in case he said "no."

"I've got a very sore throat, It's hard to speak. I feel very ill."

"Let me examine your throat. Hmm, you have a severe throat infection. I'll give you some antibiotics. What have you been doing?"

I took my prescription and left the surgery. On the way back to the hotel I bought a paper. There was a job vacancy for chambermaids and kitchen staff in Llandudno. I rang the number. I was told I could start the following Monday. I looked for the housekeeper and told her about my new job. I attempted a smile, she didn't smile back. I knew she didn't like me. She was pretending to be nice and clean. I felt breathless at the thought of travelling to my new job. I stopped at the bar and bought six packets of crisps. Once in bed I ate four packets and placed two under my pillow. I lay the used packets in front of me counting them 1,2,3,4, then again on my fingers, then on my toes. Repeating this till I managed to fall asleep. Half asleep, I heard voices. I opened my eyes a little and glanced in the direction of the noise. I could see naked arms and legs. I could hear them groaning.

"She won't wake up will she?" one of the chambermaids said.

"No, don't worry. She's off the planet that one." A young man reassured her.

I closed my eyes tight. I could smell his body, if he sees that I'm awake he'll kill me, I mustn't say anything. I gripped my mattress for safety, praying they would go away soon so I could eat my crisps.

On Friday I collected my wages, managing to get some food from the kitchen for my journey. Saturday morning I left the hotel with my carrier bag, checking the contents, my candlesticks, and photographs were still in intact. I gasped deeply for air as I left the hotel for the last time, feeling very faint as I walked towards the bus stop.

"Have you got the right time, please? Can you tell me the way to the bus stop?" I asked a passer-by, my head lowered, asking every person who passed me on the street. Arriving at the train station I paid for my ticket and waited on the platform. A young woman with a baby sat beside me. "Is this the right platform?"

"Excuse me. Did you say something?"

"No. Have you got the right time, please?"

"There's a clock over there."

"Thank you." A terrible pain shot down my arm, my chest tightened. I wanted to run but there was nowhere to go. "I'm having a heart attack." Dropping my carrier bag, I felt the pulse in my neck. There was no movement in the pulse on my wrist. "This time it is happening," I whispered. I sat on the floor next to my carrier bag.

"Are you all right?" the woman asked.

"If I was going to die would I be dead by now?" She said nothing. I gasped for air. "I'm dying. This time it's real." I whispered. I got off the floor and moved to another bench. "Have you got the right time, please?" I asked. I heard the sound of a train and looked down the tracks. How would I know it was the right train? My head was thudding. I sat near the window and huddled on the seat, I held my carrier bag tightly, and closed my eyes.

The hotel was on the promenade, I was taken to the staff quarters at the top of the building. There were no windows. It was stuffy, no way out in case of fire. I had worked three days when the housekeeper told me that I wasn't suitable for the job. Paul rang the same evening. He had been given the name of the hotel by the staff in Knutsford. He asked why I had been given the sack. I couldn't give him an answer. I didn't know why. I had very little money left. I told him I was going back to Manchester. I didn't know where I would stay. He told me he would meet me in Piccadilly Gardens. Arriving in Manchester I waited in the gardens. It was mid afternoon. I was very tired and hungry, not sure where I was going to live or what I was going to do. Perhaps he hasn't got any family. I wondered. Perhaps he needs a sister. Soon he arrived.

"Where are you going to stay?"

"I don't know." My mind felt like ice.

"I've got some money with me. We can stay in a hotel tonight." I held onto my carrier bag and followed him to a small hotel. He booked a room on the first floor.

"You're going to sleep soon, Hikey. Don't worry." I whispered. He unlocked the bedroom door and I felt comforted by the sight of the bed. I got on the bed and closed my eyes.

"What are you doing?"

"I'm going to sleep." He looked at me.

"If you don't get undressed and into bed I'll leave."

I scrambled into bed fully clothed and closed my eyes. I could smell his body as he pulled the blankets back and lay beside me. I turned away. I could hardly breathe. My body tensed. I could feel my father's finger nails, digging and scraping my flesh. My mind flashed back, I could see my father standing naked, the dark triangle between his legs. I shook my head to make it disappear.

"I'll take you back to my parent's house. I want you to be my girlfriend." I lay deadly still.

What have I done wrong? Why was he doing this to me? "Don't worry Hikey you can go to sleep soon." I whispered. My body trembled uncontrollably. Soon I fell asleep.

CHAPTER 4

I opened my eyes. Cold autumn sun was shining through the curtains onto the bedroom wall. I was alone in bed. The door was open. My heart was pounding. Feelings of emptiness crippled me. I ran along the corridor. "He's gone." Just like Jeffery, David and mum. "Mummy, mummy." I cried. The wall felt comforting as I touched it. My head felt numb as I walked back to the room.

"What are you doing?" Paul was closing the bedroom door.

"Please leave it open," I begged.

"No, I don't want people looking in." My heart started racing.

"Are you taking me home with you?"

"Yes, we'll go later. I'm going out to get some cigarettes. Do you smoke?"

"No. Please can I come with you?"

"You stay here." I wanted to run after him, knowing he wouldn't come back. Rushing to the bedroom window, looking around he was nowhere to be seen. He was gone. I ran out onto the landing crying, unable to breathe. I could hear footsteps and voices. It wasn't him. Noticing the light switch, I clicked it on and off, it felt so comforting. I got into bed and tried to sleep.

"You'll be alright, Hikey. Go to *shloff*." I closed my eyes. My body shook at the sound of the door banging.

"Here's a sandwich for you." I ate it hurriedly.

"Are we going to your house?" I asked. "I'm Jewish, not English." I whispered to myself. "I mustn't tell him." I checked my carrier bag, we left the hotel.

"We'll look around the shops. It's best if we arrive at my house late when they're all in bed."

My heart sank. I knew they wouldn't want me there.

"Are you sure you won't have a cigarette?"

"No. Jewish girls don't smoke." I whispered repeatedly to myself.

"Where do your parents and family live?"

"I don't have any."

"You're Jewish, aren't you?" I didn't answer, my heart raced. I felt light headed. My lungs needed to be filled with air, gasping deeply I held the wall. "I know you're Jewish." I remained silent. It was very late when we arrived at his home town of Seacombe. We walked past rows of small terraced houses. It was like Salford.

"What if they won't let me in?" I desperately wanted to sleep.

"Come on." I followed him, very quietly, so they wouldn't hear me. I knew they wouldn't like me. I didn't know where I would go. We crept up the stairs. He pushed the bedroom door open. I sank into the small bed and closed my eyes. "Don't go to sleep."

I lay frozen once again. It was impossible to sleep, every second of the night that passed, I waited for someone to push the door open and tell me to get out. In the morning I heard footsteps creaking on the stairs. I waited listening, pushing the blankets away before creeping down stairs. I went into the kitchen. A middle aged short stocky woman was standing in front of the fire. She backed away when she saw me, making the sign of the cross on her body. I didn't understand. It frightened me. She sat down, saying something to herself, rocking sideways as if in pain.

"My mother's never met a Jew before. Sit down. I'll make a cup of tea."

"She can't stay here. We don't have enough room. She'll bring us bad luck."

I closed my eyes and ears to what they were saying, wondering where I would be sleeping tonight. I heard a man's voice as he rushed down the stairs. I froze when he appeared in the kitchen.

"I've seen the Angel of Death upstairs. It's because she's a Jew. We'll have to move from here. She can't stay. Don't stand near to her. She'll have to go home. She belongs with her own kind." His face was reddened, his movements erratic. "Get her out."

Paul dashed over to me. "Come on. We'll have to go and look for a flat."

"Son, listen to what I'm telling you. Mark my words," his father shouted.

We left the house. My heart stopped and I stamped my foot on the ground to get it going. We searched around the town centre for shops advertising flats or bedsits to rent. The hours were passing. I was very tired and hungry. We waited for the chip shop to open, I ate my food quickly. My body felt too tired to breath. It was late evening and we began walking back towards his home.

"You stay here." I leaned on the wall for support and comfort, waiting for him. He beckoned me towards the house. My legs felt like jelly, I didn't think I would be able to move. "You can stay here till we find a flat."

I walked down the hall, up the stairs to the bedroom.

Weeks passed. Each morning we had to leave the house at six o'clock, before his family got up. That way they wouldn't be reminded they had a Jew living in the house. I would sit upstairs listening to the arguments. We weren't allowed back in the house till seven in the evening when his family had moved from the front room to the back living-room where they watched the television.

I managed to find a part-time job working in a local meat processing factory, sealing tubs of warm lard. Paul started work in a pub. We managed to find a bedsit. I made an appointment at the doctor's. I felt very ill, my throat was hot and raw, my body so weak I thought I would die. I could feel myself shaking as I walked towards the surgery, the same sense of anticipation that I had always felt, overcame me. I waited patiently, counting the seats, the leaflets hanging on the rack on the wall. I was very hungry. My name was called. I lowered my head at the mention of my name, I knocked on the doctor's door.

"Come in." I half smiled at her then looked away quickly. I sat down when she invited me to.

"What's the problem?"

"My throat's very sore. I've got a bad chest as well. I get very sick in the morning. I can't eat."

"Are you vomiting?"

"Yes. When I see or smell food."

"Have you missed your periods?"

"Yes."

"Are you taking the pill?"

I thought about what she had asked. The only pills I could think of were insulin, Duraphet and Asprin tablets. "Do you mean Asprin?"

"No. I mean the contraceptive pill," she looked at me. "Do you know what they are?"

"No."

"Did you know you could get pregnant?"

"No."

A pregnancy test was arranged and came back positive. I finished work and waited for Paul to come home. I paced the floor and kept looking out of the window for him. "I'm going to have a baby." I said as he walked through the door. He looked at me. I could see he was angry.

"I'm going out!" I followed him down the stairs to the front door. He walked off down the street. I went upstairs. Looking out of the window, crying. "Where have you gone? I want my mummy." Soon I got into bed wanting to sleep. The thoughts going around my head wouldn't stop. My head filled with all the terrible feelings of cold, damp and hunger. I pulled the blankets over me and curled up into a ball.

It was the early hours of the morning when he returned.

"Wake up! I opened my eyes. "It isn't mine." He grabbed my arm. "It isn't, is it?"

"It is."

My arm was hurting, I tried to pull away. He was too strong. He lay on the bed, I listened to him snoring, not knowing what I would do. In the morning he woke early.

"Come on. We're going to see my parents. They should know what to do." He said nothing on the way there. My heart was pounding. We passed a chip shop, the stale lingering smell of the food made me heave. I couldn't stand up straight. His mother was in the kitchen making breakfast. I could smell his father's body wafting out of the kitchen.

"I don't want her in this house," his father shouted.

"Go outside and sit on the wall. I won't be long," Paul said. I could hear raised voices.

"You'll have to marry her. You *stupid* boy." His father shouted.

"No," he replied.

"I warned you what would happen. You'll marry her."

"Come on." Paul rushed past me. "Are you going to work?"

"No. I've got the sack." I replied.

It was time for my first antenatal appointment at the hospital. I waited in a large room along with about ten other women. My name was called. The nurse led me to a small room.

"Stand on the scales." She looked at me. "How many jumpers are you wearing?"

"Four."

"Four, that's unusual. Why do you need all those jumpers?"

"I'm very cold."

"Take them off. I can't weigh you with them on. What's that on your neck? It looks like a skin infection." She examined it more closely. "It's seeping, you need to see a doctor."

I arrived back at the flat. The landlord was collecting the rents.

"I've been to the hospital. I'm having a baby."

"You can't stay here if you're pregnant, you'll have to leave." He replied. I felt frightened. I watched as he left the room. I got into bed and waited for Paul to come home. I heard him talking to someone on the landing.

"I've been to the hospital." He looked at me.

"We're getting married in six weeks time." He looked very angry. "I can fucking do without this!"

"The landlord's been for the rent, we've got to move out."

"What!" he shouted.

"I told him I'm having a baby."

"Why did you tell him that, are you stupid?"

"I'm sorry." He grabbed me by my arm, pulling me to my feet.

"I'm going out. You'd better not follow me. I'm eighteen years old, I don't need this. I don't know who you've been with. Jews do it with anyone." My arm ached, his fingers sinking deeper into my skin. "I'm off and *don't* follow me."

"Please, don't go." I listened as he went down the stairs, the front door slammed, running to the window I watched as he disappeared down the street. I walked around the room, holding my tummy, "mummy, mummy." I wanted to eat, it was impossible even the thought of food made me retch. I got on the bed and pushed my trousers down. There was no blood, there hadn't been for some time. I felt very miserable. I heard a click. The electric had run out and there was no money left to put in the meter. It was getting very dark outside, standing near the window I watched to see if he was on his way back. My heart pounding, I started shaking. There was no way of finding relief without food or sleep. I couldn't close my eyes not knowing if he was coming back. All night I paced the floor, my chest so tight the air couldn't reach my lungs, my head so full. I held my breasts for warmth and comfort. Hearing a noise I rushed to the door, opening it. It was dark. I could see the front door. Maybe he had been in and was having a cigarette outside. I wanted to go and see but was petrified by the dark.

When I woke in the morning, Paul was fast asleep at the bottom of the bed. "I'm going to work. I'm not going to work to keep you and someone else's baby. Get a job or get down to the Social Security."

I left the house. I gasped for air, stopping for a moment inhaling deeply. "I'd better go back to the flat." I started walking back, unable to breathe. My legs wouldn't support me. Have you got the right time please?" My life was ebbing away. "Please, I'm dying." I told a passer-by. She kept on walking. "Have you got the right time, please?" I asked another person. I carried on gasping for air. Nothing worked. Leaning on the wall I managed to get back to the flat. I crept up the stairs on all fours, afraid I wouldn't have enough breath or energy in my body to allow me to reach the flat. My hand was shaking uncontrollably as I put the key into the lock. I pushed the door open and rushed to the bed. "Go to *shloff*, Hikey." I whispered, holding myself tightly. The sound of the front door slamming woke me. I looked towards the window. It was getting dark outside. The bedroom door opened.

"We'll have to stay with my parents until we get a Council flat."

My tummy and breasts were getting bigger by the day. The rest of my body was getting thinner. Even the iron tablets I took instantly came back. On the day of the wedding I heaved from the moment I awoke. I crept downstairs so I wouldn't wake the family. I stood near the front door to stop the sickness and noticed the phone box across the road. I wanted to ring David or Auntie Doris but I knew there was no point. I wore a purple smock that I had bought from the market. I sat on the couch to try to summon up enough energy to get me through the day. It was time for us to walk down the road to the Registry office. The atmosphere wasn't a happy one as we walked towards the sombre looking office.

"You should have marked my words, son. You've made your bed. You have to take responsibility." The ceremony was soon over, the four of us walked back towards the house.

"I'll get fish and chips," his father said. We followed him into the shop. The smell of the food made me heave violently. I ran out. His father handed me my portion. I watched as they sat at the table, I was unable to eat. I was desperate to sleep but I knew his father wouldn't allow us to stay in the house during the day. He handed Paul a packet of cigarettes. "That's your wedding present. I'm short of money. Get onto the council this afternoon. It's about time they sorted a flat for you. The Angel of Death's still upstairs. It's not going to go until she does. Do you hear, son?"

"Yes, Dad. We'll go to the offices now."

Soon after, we received a letter from the housing department. A flat had become vacant in a place called Leasowe and we arranged to pick up the key. I had an appointment at the antenatal clinic that morning. It was at the maternity hospital close by. We made our way to the flat.

"This is it." He unlocked the front door into a tiny hall, which led to the living-room. There were two bedrooms, a bathroom and kitchen. The flat was painted pillar box red and bottle green. I didn't mind, this was my new home. We needed a cooker and a bed. Paul bought them from a second-hand shop along with two easy chairs which were delivered the same afternoon. I was now six months pregnant. Paul was still working in the factory. A week after we had moved into the flat, he came home at lunchtime. Walking into the living-room he looked at me. "I don't see why I should work to give you and *it* my money. I've handed my notice in. I didn't want to get married. This is all your fault. Get to the Benefits office."

He stormed out of the flat banging all the doors. I rushed to the window, my body crumbling in case he didn't come back. I went to bed and curled up. Later I heard the front door slam. My heart started pounding.

"Get out of bed. Why are you in bed?"

"I don't know."

"The baby's not mine is it? You tricked me into marrying you." I didn't say anything. I stayed still. "I don't want to be married." He yelled at me. Grabbing my arm, his grip was like iron. He clenched his fist and forced it towards my face, stopping short before striking me. His fist rested on my cheek.

"You're hurting my arm." He twisted it hard, then let go.

"I'll take you to the Benefits office in the morning," he said, his face red with anger.

"OK," I replied holding my arm to stop it from hurting. I heard the front door slam again, looking out of the window, he was walking down the road. The following morning we went to the Social Security office. When we arrived back at the flat his parents were waiting outside. They wanted to see where he was living. Paul showed them around.

"We can get a grant from the Council for decorating," he told his mother. His father was looking out the window. He turned around.

"What's that on your arm?" His father reached for my arm and I pulled away, I didn't want to smell his body. "It looks badly bruised, how did you do that?"

"Don't know."

"Did Paul do it?" I didn't reply. He rushed past me into the living-room. He grabbed Paul pushing him into the bedroom.

"Don't ever let me find out that you've hit a woman again! She's pregnant." He shouted. I heard him slap Paul. "Don't do that again to anyone son!" His voice was raised.

I stayed in the kitchen till his parents left the flat.

"Why did you let my father see those bruises?" he demanded.

"I didn't."

He looked very angry. I tried to push past him to get to the safety of the bedroom. My head was pulled sideways and I was being shaken and slapped repeatedly. I prayed he would feel tired or decide to go out. He carried on slapping. I didn't try to pull away. He was too strong. He stopped and grabbed his coat from the living-room. "I'm going out!"

I picked myself off the floor. The pain was terrible, my body ached. I limped towards the bedroom. My ribs and leg hurt very badly. I gently eased myself into bed and pulled the blankets over my body. I slept. The pain woke me, I decided to sit in the living-room next to the fire. I wondered where Paul was. I desperately wanted him to come home, my tummy churning over, I lay on the floor curled up like a baby, sobbing. After a while I tried to stand up. My head ached so badly all I could do was lie down again. Later I looked out of the window. He was nowhere in sight. Perhaps he's been run over, the words going round in my head, they wouldn't stop. I saw someone walking down the path. It was Paul. I sat in the chair pleased that he had returned home. He looked at me. I wasn't sure whether or not I should smile. I could see by the look on his face he was very angry.

"Don't ever go and see my parents. They hate you because you're a Jew. They don't want you in their house. If they come here don't answer the door. Don't let them in. I don't want you showing them any bruises."

He pushed past me towards the bedroom. I waited a while, following him, desperately wanting to go to bed to sleep. He was in bed his eyes were closed I wondered if he was asleep. I put my arm around him and closed my eyes.

"It's not my baby. I know it's not." His voice made me jump, I remained silent. "You're a fucking tart."

I stayed still. He kicked me so hard that I was hanging out of the bed. His hand smashed across my face, with such force that I could see small stars flashing in front of my eyes. My face felt wet, my nose was bleeding. He managed to push me out of bed so I was lying on the floor. I needed to sleep.

"Piss off out. Get out!" He sat up and I rushed from the bedroom, I could hear his footsteps, I rushed through the hall and out of the front door. Standing outside the flat, my heart was banging, my eyes closing. "Get in here," he insisted. He was holding the front door open. I didn't know if I wanted to run away or not. I knew there was nowhere to go. I watched as he went back into the living-room. I crept through the front door. I didn't close it in case I had to run out again, frightened for myself and the baby.

The weeks passed by slowly. The beatings carried on daily. By now I was seven months pregnant. The days were very hot, the nights cold. Some nights I wasn't allowed to get into bed, on occasions I was too afraid to, I would sleep on the chair in the living-room. Paul wouldn't let me have a blanket or put the fire on. I would get very chilled sitting all night with only my clothes to keep me warm. I awoke one morning.

As usual all the doors were open in case I needed to run out of the flat to get away from him. The room was very draughty. My back ached badly as I moved in the chair. I felt hot, very weak and it was difficult to breathe. I coughed to clear my throat. My chest tightened so much it was painful to breathe. I managed to get off the chair. Each time I coughed, the pain was unbearable.

"Please, can I get into bed?" He opened his eyes, but didn't reply. I crept along the room and eased my body on the bed. I coughed uncontrollably, my chest ached, the pain in my back terrible. I held my tummy to keep the baby secure.

"I can't stand this. I'm going out," he shouted. The front door slammed. I wanted to look out of the window to see if he'd gone, it was impossible for me to move. He returned later in the day, I felt too tired and ill to notice. His father called to see him. I opened my eyes and they were both standing near the bedroom door.

"Please get the doctor. I can't breathe. I can't move."

"It's Saturday, you can't disturb the doctor on Saturday," his father replied.

"Please. I'm in agony." My eyes closed. I awoke later in the day still coughing uncontrollably, my eyes and nose streaming liquids. I could hear voices. The bedroom door opened, two ambulance men came through holding a stretcher.

"Come on." I was helped to my feet. My body and clothes soaking wet with sweat.

"When's the baby due?"

"Four weeks." I replied, grasping his arm for support. Once in the ambulance I was given oxygen. The pain was getting worse. We were on our way to the hospital. The ambulance stopped. I could see two people out of the window. The door opened and I watched as a young couple sat opposite me. The doors closed.

"We're giving our friends a lift." The ambulance driver said.

I was pleased that the ambulance man had friends so he wouldn't be lonely. Soon the ambulance stopped. I wasn't sure if I should smile at them or not. I heard them all talking and watched as they left.

"We're almost at the hospital."

The doctor examined me. "You're badly bruised."

"I fell." I was taken to the geriatric ward. Two nurses helped me into bed.

"You've got bronchial pneumonia. If there are any complications you'll have to have a caesarean." An oxygen tent was placed around my bed. I tried to lie down and sleep it was too painful, I couldn't stop coughing. I looked around. This was now my new home.

"Shut up!" One of the women shouted. I covered my mouth and tried to muffle the sound of the coughs, soon some of the old ladies were awake, hurling abuse because their sleep had been disturbed. I wanted to go home to my mum. I didn't like the hospital. I started vomiting.

"What's going on?" the nurse asked. Now all the women were complaining about the noise. She appeared with two tablets and a glass of water. I gasped for air, swallowed the tablets and soon fell asleep.

The doctor ordered complete bed rest for two weeks, till the Bronchial pneumonia had cleared. I was sent back to the flat where I waited till the baby was due. When the labour pains started I went to the maternity hospital on my own. I was lying on my bed in a small room. A drip was inserted into the vein on the back of my hand. I didn't understand what was happening. Screams were coming from the room opposite.

"Has someone had an accident?" I asked the nurse.

"No," she said, shaking her head.

I was taken to the ward, there was a young woman in the next bed, screaming, bent over in agony, ripping at the sheets. After I had the baby I was taken to a different ward. I could hear crying.

"Has someone had an accident?" I asked a different nurse.

"No, it's a young girl. She's fourteen. They must have come to take the baby away this morning. She doesn't want to part with her."

I never received any visitors.

CHAPTER 5

I returned home with the baby. He was asleep in his cot, Paul was in bed. I ran across the road to the phone box. Eagerly, I fingered my way through the telephone directory to find the nearest synagogue. I rang the number and a middle aged man answered. My heart sank. "Hello, may I help you?"

"I want my baby to have a *bris*."

"If you come to the synagogue, we can arrange it." My head was filled with terrible dark feelings, I couldn't think straight. "Hello, hello?" He repeated.

I placed the receiver down, walking away from the phone box the urge to binge and vomit was strong. "Jane Levene. Who do you think you are? I hate you. I'll teach you when we get home." I whispered. The baby was crying when I returned to the flat. Paul was sitting on the couch.

"Your baby's crying." I hurried through to the bedroom my finger on the light switch turning it on and off three times. I lifted him out of his cot. Paul followed me. "Who did you talk to?"

"Nobody."

"Slut. You were talking to a man outside the phone box."

"No, I wasn't, honestly."

"You'll go with anyone, won't you?"

Holding the baby, I felt a thud at the back of my head. I fell forward holding onto the baby. I fell on top of him.

"I'm going out. I can't stand the sight of you or *your* baby."

I ran to the bedroom window to see which direction he was going in. He might never return. My chest felt like a rope had been tightened around it. I went into the kitchen and stuffed as much food as I could manage into my mouth. I felt exhausted at the thought of having to make myself sick. I knew I had to. Standing over the toilet I stuck my fingers down my throat. "I hate you Levene." My eyes and nose streamed liquid as I retched, my head was thudding, my body felt weak. I could sense my mother and father. I could see that every last bit of food was out of my stomach. "Why did you ring the synagogue? What do you think you were doing? You're nobody." I was whimpering. The baby started crying again.

"Please don't cry." I begged. Looking at him, his eyes were closed, his face was red and bulbous, the noise was getting louder. I felt light headed, my heart pounding. "I'm useless and stupid." I told him. "A smelly baked bean. Please don't cry." I begged once more. He didn't take any notice of my words. "I know you don't like me."

His tiny body was shaking, his screams became louder. I wanted to lay over him and suffocate him. If he was dead he would never feel pain. He would never be able to leave me or dislike me. I could keep him all to myself forever. I looked at him wondering how to make him stop crying. The terrible atmosphere in my head got worse. The crying noises were getting louder and louder. I wanted him to need me badly. I knew it was never going to happen. He carried on screaming. Afraid of what I would do I rushed out of the front door and down the stairs. Walking around the block, my body shaking as I touched the wall. I went back to the flat. I bent over and lifted him out of his cot. "I love you, please don't cry. I won't hurt you." I whispered in his ear, stroking his back, feeling his warm cheek next to mine. "I'll never leave you, honest." He stopped crying. "We'll go to *shloff* for a while." I lay him next to me on the bed and we fell asleep. The front door slammed. I awoke startled. Shaking uncontrollably, I kept quiet.

"Where are you?" Paul shouted. He pushed the bedroom door open. I looked at the baby, he was still fast asleep. "I'm not giving you any money. I don't want this." I watched as he walked over to the bed. I pulled the baby close to me praying he would leave us alone. "Get out of bed."

I pushed the blankets back and stood near to the wall. I closed my eyes as I saw his fist racing towards my face, my head jerked with each slap and punch. Staying silent in the hope he would go away. He stopped. I opened my eyes when I heard the bedroom door slam. I wiped the blood from my nose. The baby started crying again. It was time for his feed. My pullover was damp where the milk seeped from my breasts. Sitting on the bed I put the baby to my breast, listening to him as he sucked and grunted at his food. I lay him on the bed and changed his nappy.

"We'll go to *shloff* now" I smiled, pulling him closer and stroking his fine hair.

A crash vibrated through the flat. Opening my eyes, my hearing became focused, my mind alert. I lifted the baby out of bed and laid him in his cot, closing his bedroom door. Paul was standing in the hall. My body froze as he lunged towards me. He was pulling my hair and punching my head, I raised my hands to stop the pain. I curled up in a ball on the floor waiting for him to stop. The front door slammed and I rushed to the window. My heart sank as he disappeared from sight. I went to the baby's room and wrapped him in a blanket. Making sure my front door key was in my pocket. I hurried out of the house.

"What have you been doing?" A woman from next door asked looking at my black eye.

"I fell."

"Looks like you've been hit." I looked away. "What did you do to deserve that?"

"I don't know."

"You must have done something," she insisted.

I tried to remember where his friend lived. I had met his mother on a few occasions. She was looking out of the window. She recognised me and waved.

"Can I come in?"

She opened the front door. I breathed a sigh of relief. I followed her into the living-room.

"Would you like a cup of tea?"

"Yes, please. He's been hitting me."

"I can see. That bruising looks nasty."

"Can I stay here for a while? Please."

"Yes. I know what it feels like. Years ago I worked for a doctor, I cleaned his house. He raped and beat me, that's how I got pregnant." She sat down sobbing. "He arranged a backstreet abortion. I almost bled to death, my son survived." She was agitated, unable to stop talking. I heard a knock on the door. I got very frightened.

"Is Jane here?" It was Paul's voice. He followed her into the living-room. "Come home, I promise I'll change." He came over to me and lifted the baby out of my arms. He handed me some money. "Here take this. Go and buy some food. I'll take the baby home."

I watched as he lifted the baby in his arms. We left the flat and he went home. Putting the key, in the lock I felt relieved that Paul had changed. He wasn't going to hit me any more.

After we had eaten, it was time to feed the baby. I sat him on my lap making sure the blanket was secure around his body. I relaxed in the chair putting the baby to my breast. Closing my eyes I squirmed as I felt the milk being drawn out of my body. "*Gehen Shloffen*" I whispered. For a while my world felt calm and comforted. Soon the baby stopped sucking and I moved him to the other breast. I smiled as his lips instinctively found my nipple, his mouth glued itself to me, sucking with all its might. I closed my eyes, stroking his head gently as he fed. Time seemed to stand still. I opened my eyes and Paul was standing beside me. I smiled at him, there was no response.

"Did you chat up some bloke when you went to the shop?"

"No."

"I don't fucking believe you. If it wasn't for me you'd still be in the gutter. Where you belong." My head lowered. I could see him walking around, agitated. "Where would you be?"

"In the gutter."

He was becoming more agitated. He started shouting, "You're a fucking moaner. She's my friend's mother. You've really embarrassed me. Don't go there again."

"OK."

I knew I had to get the baby back in his cot. My heart was racing so fast I prayed I wouldn't pass out before he was safe again. Walking towards the door that led to the bedroom I gasped for air. My lungs were failing, I didn't want my heart to stop. I leaned over the cot and placed the baby securely in it. He started crying. "I'll be back soon." I crept into the bedroom and looked out of the window to see if Paul had gone out. I tapped four times on the window sill with one hand then the other. The bedroom door lunged open, he swung his fists towards me. I covered my face and closed my eyes. My hair was being pulled. My face swung from side to side with the force of the punches. I desperately wanted to sleep. I was pushed to the floor feeling the kicks all about my body.

"You won't go moaning to anyone again, will you?"

"No, honestly."

He pulled me up by my hair and pushed me onto the bed. My eyes were still closed as I heard the door slam shut. The baby was still crying. I pulled the blankets over myself and stroked my face. "Don't worry Hikey." The sound of the baby crying woke me. I didn't want to move. Pushing the blankets away I dragged myself out of bed and opened the door. He looked at me, his face contorted, his screams pierced my ears. Pulling him to my chest, I rubbed his back he let out a loud burp that echoed around the room. I held his head gently and looked at his face, he was smiling. I lay him back in the cot. "I love you. Go to *shloff* my little one."

It was time to take the baby to the antenatal clinic. It was at the bottom of the road. I was told he was making good progress. As I walked out of the clinic a young woman with a baby approached me. "I remember you from hospital. What have you done to your face?"

"I knocked it on the kitchen cupboard."

She rolled her sleeve up to her elbow and showed me her bruises. "He never hits me in the face. It's always hidden. Why don't you come for a cup of tea? I live around the corner."

"I'll try to come later."

The flat was similar to mine. I knocked on the door.

"Come in, don't let the dog out."

There was dog shit all over the floor. The flat was very warm and the smell was overpowering. Three young children were running around half naked. The baby was lying in an open cradle. She wasn't wearing a nappy and the sheet was the colour of stale urine. The baby's bottom was covered in large open red sores, she was screaming. "They want to take the kids and put them in care. I don't want that, I was always in homes when I was a kid. You never knew where they were gonna stick you."

Walking home, I felt very frightened. What if they wanted to take my baby away? I stopped at the newsagents and bought an evening paper. I saw an advert for a live-in housekeeper in a different area. One child would be acceptable. I found the nearest phone box and rang the number making an appointment for the following day. I was so desperate to sleep, my eyes were closing. I rushed home.

As I approached the property I could see it was a large shop with a flat above it. The road was tree lined and quiet.

"I've come about the job. I rang yesterday."

"Wait upstairs," a middle aged man said. My tummy churned so badly I held it. I felt sick. I heard his footsteps on the stairs.

"Have you done any housekeeping before?"

"Yes, I worked in lots of hotels in the Lake District. I was a chambermaid."

"I might need you to help in the shop at times. What do you think?"

"Yes, I don't mind. I can't use scales" I said desperately. He sat back on the chair. I moved away from him.

"If I'm relaxed after having a shower and I feel like having sex with you, I expect no arguments."

I felt frightened. I looked over at the living-room door. I picked up the baby and pushchair. "I've got to go now. Thank you." As I walked hurriedly down the road I couldn't forgive myself for hurting him, I knew he was lonely. The urge to go back was terrible but I carried on walking.

The weeks turned to months. The situation didn't change. I awoke early one morning to the sound of the baby crying. I opened my eyes, Paul wasn't there. I tried to move my arms, it was almost impossible, terrible pain travelled up my arms. My breasts were very hot and painful, full of lumps. The baby was still crying. "I won't be long." I tried to calm him down and holding my breasts, I slowly eased myself out of bed. I managed to get the baby out of his cot and pushed him around the corner to the doctor's surgery.

The doctor examined me. "You're suffering from mastitis. Your breasts are in a terrible state."

I started crying. "My husband makes fun of them. Calls me names, my back aches all the time."

"I think something needs to be done. Have you considered plastic surgery? Would you like me to refer you to a consultant?"

"Yes, please."

The infection cleared up. I received an appointment to see the consultant. He agreed with the doctor that the size of my breasts needed to be reduced. I had the operation. Over the next few weeks the violence at home ceased. The beatings started again when the scars began to heal

Each night I would go to bed after I had made sure that all the doors were left slightly open so that I could get out quickly. One evening I decided to go to bed very early. The baby was fast asleep in his cot and I was desperate to sleep. I closed my eyes. The silence was broken by a crashing noise.

Sitting up in bed my heart pounding, the bedroom door flew open and Paul stood there staring at me.

"I'm not giving you any more money, you can get a job. I'm starting work on Monday. I'm not working to keep you and him."

"OK," I agreed so he wouldn't get angry. My body tensed. I closed my eyes and remained silent as he dragged me to the floor punching and kicking, pulling my clothes off.

"Why do you fucking wear so many jumpers?"

I said nothing and kept my eyes closed because of the blood, feeling my way I crept towards the bedroom door. He pulled me back. My head was aching where he was pulling my hair. I could feel some had been pulled out by the roots. My face shot from side to side with the force of his fists punching me. I lay still until he had finished punching and kicking. I crept out of the bedroom and into the living-room.

All the doors were open and I ran out of the flat barely dressed and crossed the road to the phone box. I rang 999.

"Please help me."

"What's the problem?"

"My husband's hitting me." I said, my whole body shaking.

"Give me your name and address. I'll send an officer to see you."

I waited in the hall too frightened to go back into the living-room or bedroom. The policeman arrived.

"My husband's been hitting me. I'm frightened" I told him pacing to and fro in the hall. I opened my coat. "Look." I showed him the redness and bruising.

"All I can do is to take you to a hostel, but that's only for one night."

The living-room door opened and Paul appeared. "I'm sorry, I won't do it again. Don't worry officer."

The policeman left the flat, closing the door. I opened it again. Perhaps now the beatings would stop. I crept into the bedroom Paul was asleep. "*Shama Yisroel*, perhaps God will make him sleep till the morning."

"That baby's not mine" You're not getting another penny off me. I didn't want to get married," he shouted.

"OK."

The following morning I fed and dressed the baby and we made the short journey into town, to look for work. I picked out a few jobs at the employment centre. They were all part-time. The one in the cake factory looked the best. It wasn't far from the flat and the hours were six in the evening till ten o'clock. A young woman interviewed me.

"It's packing cakes and working on the conveyor belt."

"As long as there are no scales or numbers."

She looked at the card. "No, it's just packing. Would you like me to give them a ring?"

"Yes please." I looked around while she was chatting.

"Tuesday, Wednesday, Thursday and Friday, is that OK?"

"Yes, thank you."

"You can start next Tuesday. They'll provide you with overalls."

"Thanks." I was still holding the pushchair handle.

"I've got a job. I'll look after you." I whispered to the baby. I took the details off the woman and we went home. Paul was out.

"We'll go to *shloff*." I lay the baby on the bed near to the wall. He was chuckling and waving his arms about. I lay beside him, tickling his tummy. I was woken by the sound of the front door slamming. I sat up, my heart pounding. The baby started pulling at my coat.

"Where are you?" Before I could answer he entered the room.

"I've got a job." I tried to smile but my whole body was shaking with fear. He lunged towards me. "Please, leave me alone," I begged.

"No, you tricked me into marrying you." I could feel the baby's hand on my leg and tried desperately to get out of the bed and run away. I couldn't battle against Paul's strength. "You're a tart. You'd be in the gutter if it wasn't for me. Nobody wanted you. Your fucking family couldn't give a shit about you. Why do you think that is?"

I remained silent, the slaps to my face prevented me from replying. Opening my eyes, my body huddled in a ball for protection. The kicks to my body were coming fast and furious. The bedroom door closed and I opened my eyes. Paul had gone. The baby was crying, his arms outstretched towards me. My body ached as I crawled towards the bed. I lay down beside him, holding his tiny hand. The bedroom door flew open. Paul reached towards me, grabbing the pillow from under my head. I couldn't breathe. He held the pillow tightly over my face. I struggled to get it off, the baby needed me. I couldn't let myself die. My heart was banging as I gasped for any amount of air my body could take in. He let go of the pillow and I pushed it away, spluttering, gasping for air. I held the baby close and listened to hear the front door slam shut. Getting the baby out of the flat, I hurried to his friend's mother's flat. The main door to the flats was open and I banged on her door.

"Please can I come in?" I begged. My body so tense it was difficult to breathe.

She appeared, holding a wet flannel. I held it to my lips and nose, trying to stop the bleeding. "Can I stay here for a while? I'm very tired."

"Yes, I'll put the kettle on." The hours passed. I was falling in and out of sleep on the couch. "You can sleep on the couch when I go to bed." There was a knock on the door.

"Is Jane here?" It was Paul. He sat down beside me. I could feel my heart pounding. "Come home, please, It won't happen again. I've learnt my lesson, I promise."

I half smiled at him and looked for the baby's coat. It stayed calm that evening. I put the baby in his cot and he soon fell asleep. Paul was in the living-room watching the television. I sat down near him. I smiled at him but there was no response.

"What will your wage be?"

"I don't know, enough to buy food for me and the baby."

"You must know how much you're going to get?"

I stayed silent trying hard to remember if I had left the front door open. My neck shook. He punched the side of my face with such force I could see bright white stars before my eyes. I knew the position of my nose had changed. I was being dragged across the room by my hair. I tried desperately to pull away, his hands clasped around my arms, it was impossible. The kicks vibrated through the whole of my body. I was hoping he would soon get tired and go to bed. I heard the door close, I looked up and he was gone. I ran across the road to the phone box. Once again I rang the police. "Please help me. I don't know what to do. He's going to kill me." I walked back towards the flat, staying outside until I saw the police car. The policeman followed me into the flat.

"I can take you to the hostel, you can stay overnight. There's nothing else I can do."

"That's what I was told the last time but he won't stop hitting me."

Paul appeared. "It won't happen again." He told the policeman.

The following morning I awoke early. My body so tense it was almost impossible to move. Gasping for breath, I woke Paul.

"Shut up," he shouted, pushing and kicking me till I got out of bed.

I looked in the baby's room, he was awake and I fed him. It was nine o'clock. I combed my hair and walked around the corner to the doctor's surgery. I waited until my name was called. It was a new doctor. I knew straight away he was Jewish.

"Sit down," he said, in broken English.

"Please can I go back to see the surgeon at the hospital?" I begged.

"Why?" Looking surprised, he fingered through my medical notes.

"I need to have my nose straightened."

"I see you've had a breast operation."

"Yes, there were people in the hospital having their nose straightened."

"You're Jewish. I see your maiden name was Levene."

"Please can I go and see him? I don't want people to know I'm Jewish."

"What, you want to look like a *shiksa*? Get out. Go home. I've never heard such nonsense. You're wasting my time." He pointed towards the door and I left the room.

I waited at the bus stop. The hospital wasn't far away and I knew I had to go and see the surgeon. I felt light headed, my heart pounding as I walked up the path that led to the reception area. I tried hard to keep my lungs full of air so I wouldn't die.

"Can I speak to the plastic surgeon?" I asked the receptionist.

"Do you have an appointment?"

"No."

"You can't see him without an appointment."

"Alright." My heart still pounding, I walked down the corridor, my head held down, wondering where I would start looking for him. Two men were talking. I looked closer. They were standing outside the operating theatre, both dressed in white outfits and white boots, covered in blood. I recognised one of them, he was the surgeon who had operated on me. I walked up to them.

"Excuse me, please." They both looked at me.

"Please, will you straighten my nose for me?" I begged. They both carried on looking.

"Haven't you recently had a breast operation?" the surgeon asked.

"Yes." Tears started flooding down my cheeks. "Please. I don't want anyone to know I'm Jewish."

He paused for a while. "You know, if you have psychological problems they won't go away if you have your nose straightened."

"Please, I'll give you two shillings a week for the rest of my life, to pay for it. I promise. It's a Jewish nose. I'm frightened of people knowing I'm Jewish." He stood silent. I thought he would never reply. "Please."

"I'll do it, but you can't keep having plastic surgery on the National Health Service."

"I only want this. Thank you. I'll never ask for anything ever again."

He examined my nose. "This is a typical Jewish nose. Do you want this part removing? It's known as a Jews droop, I can turn your nose up at the end."

"No, thank you. I just want it straight." I tried to raise a smile at him, my head still slightly lowered.

"I'll contact you when the nurses strike is over."

The following week I started work at the cake factory at six p.m. The room was huge, the vats for mixing the cake mixture were very big. There were people everywhere doing different jobs. Everyone knew what to do. As I joined them I watched what they were doing. I was given a white overall and hat. I was shown to the conveyor belt and told what to do. The sight of all the cakes made me very hungry and I wished I could eat them all. Soon it was time for a tea break and the conveyor belts were turned off.

"Get yourself a cake, bring it to the canteen."

I picked up a family size pineapple cake and a butter cream cake. I followed the other women to the canteen. I found a small table where I could sit on my own and started eating. After eating the cakes my head felt heavy with dark feelings, I felt so weak I knew I had to get everything out of my tummy. I went back to work, taking the freshly baked cakes and placing them on a large trolley.

"Choc Shop," someone shouted. I looked around and could see a small bird flying near the roof of the building.

"What's that? What's choc shop?" I asked one of the women.

"When a bird craps on the cakes it goes on that trolley over there. They're sold in the choc shop for the staff. They're cheap. You want to go and have a look after work."

I had been working for a few weeks. Each evening I worked I would leave the flat at five thirty knowing Paul was home looking after the baby. One night I returned from work, Paul had gone out. The following morning, I heard a loud knock at the front door. It was a policeman.

"Do you know you almost had your baby taken away last night?" He said sternly. I looked at him, trembling, crying uncontrollably.

"No."

"Well you went out, then your husband went out, it was reported to us at seven o'clock by a neighbour. If the baby had been crying when we arrived, we would have broken down the door and taken him away, you're very lucky."

I couldn't control the tears as I listened to what he was saying. "I didn't know my husband was going out, he said he would to stay in and look after the baby."

"OK. We'll leave it this time."

I closed the front door. Paul was sitting in the living-room. "Why did you leave him alone?"

"He's your baby, you look after him."

A few weeks later I went into hospital to have the nose operation.

CHAPTER 6

My body tensed in fear as I heard the front door open. My eyes remained fixed on the television, my hands caressed the baby's arms as he lay gurgling on my lap. He was eighteen months old.

"What are you doing?" Paul asked.

I stayed silent and stiff, hoping he would go into the bedroom. My heart started banging as I realised he was glaring at me. I looked down at the baby smiling. "I love you." I whispered stroking him.

"I *said* what are you doing?" My chest tightened. I felt my pulse to see if I was still alive. I stamped my foot on the floor to make sure I wasn't dying, leaving the baby without a mother.

"Put the baby in his cot. *Now!*" Paul shouted.

My heart was pounding. I looked in the direction of the living-room door to see if it was slightly open so I could get out quickly. It was getting dark. I lay the baby in his cot, covering his little body with the blankets. "Go to *shloff.*" I closed the door.

"Get in here." I pushed the bedroom door open. Paul was lying on the bed. "What are you doing?"

"Nothing."

"You're good at doing nothing."

"I'm going to check the front doors locked. I won't be a minute." I walked to the door and opened it slightly.

"Get in here!" He shouted. I got into bed and felt comforted by the clothes I was wearing. I was relieved when he fell asleep.

I wrapped my arms around myself. The silence was broken by the loud vibration of his voice. "You're a slut." I kept my eyes closed and stayed very still. "You're a tart. What are you?"

"A tart."

"Where would you be if it wasn't for me?"

"In the gutter."

"Take your clothes off." He pulled at my jumper. I remained silent as he pulled the jumper over my head. "Get out of bed." He shouted, shaking my body and kicking my legs.

I felt too frightened to say or do anything. I only wanted to sleep.

"Piss off." He yelled. My heart was pounding. Each thump on my back made me gasp for air. "Fuck off." His voice insistent, he knelt beside me. I tried to stay on the bed. He was too strong for me to fight, pushing me off the bed onto the floor. "You're dirt." He laughed.

I noticed the pattern on the sole of his boot as he kicked my face. I lay curled up on the floor trying to protect myself from the barrage of kicks. The pain was unbearable. I picked myself off the floor, deciding to sleep on the floor in the baby's room.

"Where do you think you're going?" I turned to look at him and stayed silent, my body shaking with fear.

"Come here." He beckoned, lying on the bed.

I shook my head. "No."

He sat on the side of the bed. I froze for a moment then felt his hand on my head, pulling my hair. I could feel the hair stretching at the roots as he dragged me towards him. His face frenzied, his grip like steel.

"You're a Jew slut aren't you?"

"Yes." I replied, trying to pull away.

The side of my head hit the wall as he pushed me. My face felt numb as he slapped me with great force. I stayed very still against the wall, holding it, gaining some comfort from it. I watched as drop after drop of blood fell from my nose, hitting the floor. Another punch in the face made me hit out at him. His eyes opened so wide as he lunged towards me. Kicking and thumping. I managed to get out of the bedroom as the bedroom door slammed behind me. I sat on the floor, beside the door, my face throbbing, trembling with cold and fear. I managed to stand and staggered towards the baby's room. The door flew open and Paul lunged towards me. This time he stayed silent.

My body shook with the first kick to my naked body. His boots were heavy. First he kicked at my legs. Then my thighs, I curled in a ball to try to protect myself, his kicks penetrated me, the bones in my back and ribs felt like they were crumbling. I knew I was going to die. Screams echoed around the room as I tried to reach up to the window so I could jump out. He pulled me back and carried on kicking and slapping. After a while he got tired of it and went into the bedroom, closing the door behind him.

I looked at the baby, relieved he hadn't been harmed. I managed to get off the floor. A sense of calm came over me. I went into the kitchen and found a sharp knife. Stabbing at the wall, slashing the curtains, ripping into the sofa, suddenly I had all the energy I needed. Rushing to the bedroom I stabbed the door with all my might. He opened the door and I faced him. He closed the door quickly, sitting behind it.

"Put the knife down!" he shouted.

"No, I'll kill you if you come out here." I shouted, my arms finding the energy to carry on stabbing at the door, my voice soon becoming exhausted.

He stayed behind the door using his weight to keep it closed, remaining silent. I crawled to the baby's room and laid the knife down. My heart was pounding making it difficult to inhale enough air to keep me alive. I tried harder, knowing the baby needed me. He was standing in his cot holding the rails tightly in each hand gurgling happily, oblivious to what was happening around him. He smiled at me and I smiled back, reaching up to stroke his hands, waiting a few minutes till I was absolutely sure my heart was still beating.

"I'll never leave you." I used the cot rails to help me to stand. I leaned over to him, careful not to press my bruised body on the cot. "Come on." Quietly I lifted him out of his cot. "Mummy loves you."

I held him with one arm and picked what few clothes he had off the floor then crept very quietly towards the living-room. Each door was open so I made little noise. Still holding the baby I leaned over and picked up a carrier bag lying in the corner of the room, stuffing his clothes in it. The rent book was on the sideboard with a five pound note. I grabbed it and made quietly for the hall leading to the front door. My shoes were in the living-room. Putting my coat on over my naked body and fumbling to make sure all the buttons were fastened. I grabbed the baby's anorak and pushchair, hurrying out of the flat, down the stairs and out of the main front door. The cold air made my body tense and even more painful.

"Don't worry." I sobbed, dashing into the first available entry, so I could dress him more warmly. I put his coat on. I dropped the carrier bag and moved the pushchair to one side. Kneeling down I placed the baby on my knees. Managing to find a baby grow and put it on over the one he was already wearing. Then put his coat back on, tucking his small blanket under his legs. I pulled his hood over his head and kissed his cheek. "You'll be nice and warm now," I reassured him. He replied with a gurgling smile. "We'll ring Auntie Doris, to see if we can stay with her for a while."

I tried to remember where the nearest phone box was. I looked through my pockets for some change. It was very dark and cold. I wondered what time it was. I dialled Auntie Doris's number, my heart stopped. I stamped my foot on the ground. I must keep myself alive, if I'm going to look after the baby. The phone was ringing, I felt faint as I heard the receiver being lifted.

"Who is this?"

"It's Jane." The whole of my body shook. "Please can I stay with you for a while? Just for a few nights? Till I find somewhere to live. My husband's been hitting me. I have a baby."

"It's two o'clock in the morning." There was deadly silence. "No, I don't want you here. Anyway, you might not go." She hung up.

I reached for the pushchair. The baby was warmly tucked up under his blanket. I walked along the streets looking for another back entry where we could shelter till the morning without being seen. I stayed close to the walls touching them. Arranging the pushchair so it was out of sight, I knelt beside it keeping my gaze on the sky. It was starting to get a little lighter. My eyes closed a few times. I tried to keep awake so we wouldn't miss the first bus. The sound of a milk float woke me. Making my way to the bus stop, the baby opened his eyes and closed them again. I prayed he would sleep. The five pound note was still firmly placed in my coat pocket. I lifted the baby out of the pushchair, managing to clamber onto the bus holding him and my possessions tightly.

He started whimpering, I knew he was hungry and hoped he would fall asleep until we reached the bus station. As the bus stopped I looked out of the window, a café was open. The baby was crying. I tried to tell him he would soon be able to eat. I hurried to the café. Ordering two cups of tea and four pieces of toast I sat the baby on my lap, pulling his hood back, I kept one arm firmly around his little body helping him to eat his toast.

"Don't cry. I'll look after you."

"Isn't she pretty with those long black eyelashes." a woman said as she walked past the table.

"He's a boy."

"What have you done to your face?"

"Nothing."

She walked away. "What have you done to your face?" I kept repeating over and over. The bus journey seemed to last forever. Feeling drowsy I felt I wanted sleep and not wake up. The baby started crying.

"Go to *shloff*." I whispered cuddling him, he didn't want to sleep, he wanted to play, tugging at my coat, smiling. "Don't worry." I pressed my face against his.

We arrived in Manchester. I wondered what we would do and where we would go. My head was full of cold piercing feelings that penetrated my whole body. I collected my belongings and stepped off the bus. Securing the pushchair I placed the baby firmly in it. "What are we going to do?"

I walked out of the bus station, not knowing what was going to happen. A young policeman was approaching me. I stopped him.

"I haven't got anywhere to stay." He thought for a moment.

"You're best going to the Homeless Families department in Piccadilly." He pointed to a building across the road.

"Thank you." I smiled, quickly lowering my head and started walking. It was a large multi-storey building, grey and bleak. It reminded me of the National Assistance office. Once in the building I could smell smoke. I listened to see if I could hear crackling wood. I felt my heart stop and stamped my foot on the ground, it started to work again. I was directed to the office. A middle aged woman sat behind the desk. "Is this the Homeless Families department?"

"Yes, can I help you?"

"I've left my husband, he was hitting me and we haven't got anywhere to go."

"Where is the marital home?"

"Liverpool but I come from Manchester."

"How long have you lived away from Manchester?"

"About four years." My tummy churned over and over.

"In that case I can only give you the fare to go back to the marital home, you're not our responsibility."

"I can't go back. He's hitting me." She looked at the bruising on my face. I opened my coat, showing her my bruised naked body. "I can't go back. He'll kill us."

"I'll ring around the hostels. They won't take you if you've been living out of the area for over three years." She lifted the receiver. My mind went numb as I watched her lips, her every movement, then she placed the phone down. "There are no places. All I can offer you is your fare back to the marital home. If you were black or Irish, if you had just stepped off a plane I could help. Do you want your fare?"

"No, I can't go back. I'll have to walk the streets all night."

"Well if you do that, you will be put in the cells and charged with vagrancy and your baby will be taken into care."

I made sure my coat was fastened properly and started pushing the baby out of the office. In the corridor I counted my money. The baby whimpered and moved around in the pushchair, his leg was wet. I headed for the nearest public toilet so I could change his nappy. It felt warm and secure in the toilets. I wished we could live there. My eyes kept closing, I knew I dare not fall asleep. I started walking in the direction of Cheetham Hill Road. Noticing a phone box I decided to ring Mrs Roth. The phone started ringing I hoped she would answer, not her husband. I didn't want to smell him. It frightened me.

"Hello?" I recognised the voice straight away, it was Mrs Roth.

"It's Jane Levene, Mrs. Roth. I've got a baby." There was silence.

"I can't talk to you now, I'm busy."

"Alright, Mrs Roth," I replied, smiling I put the receiver back in its place. I walked past the old surgery on Cheetham Hill Road, deciding I would go to see Auntie Doris to ask her again if we could stay, perhaps for one night. I went into a nearby shop and bought the baby a bar of chocolate. It was a long walk I knew the baby would be hungry. As I approached my father's flat I crossed the road. I didn't want to look at it or have to smell his body. My body trembled.

I was so tired I wanted to run into someone's garden, curl up and fall asleep. I carried on walking pushing the baby and touching the wall for comfort. I stopped to take a look at him. He was fast asleep. Greenhill Road was in sight, I started to feel breathless and light headed. Stamping my foot on the ground and waiting a few minutes till I was sure everything was working properly. Auntie Doris's door was in sight. The baby was crying, I lifted him out of his pushchair and held him close to my chest. I stepped onto the first step and banged on the door. My heart stopped. I moved near to the wall in case I fainted. The door opened. Uncle Asher was standing there.

"What do you want?" I couldn't speak, I could smell him. "Your hair's blonde, you look like a *shiksa*, what do you want?"

"We haven't got anywhere to stay."

"You can't stay here. Go away, people might think we're having non-Jewish visitors. You made your bed, now lie in it." He slammed the door.

Sitting on the step, I put the baby back in his pushchair wondering where we would go. "Maybe the Sarah Laski Home, they may let us stay for one night." I whispered, "for one night" I repeated over and over till my head hurt.

The home was about an hour away. I fought the need to curl up on the steps and sleep. Soon, the Sarah Laski Home was in sight. My body trembled with terrible feelings. I knew I had to carry on till I got there. Shaking, I knocked on the door. A young woman opened the front door. I wasn't sure if she was the Matron.

"Are you the Matron?"

"No."

"Please can I speak to the Matron?" I tried to raise a smile holding onto the pushchair for support.

"What's it about?" I started crying.

"Please can I see the Matron?"

She beckoned me in, telling me to wait for the Matron outside her office. I looked in noticing that all the furniture was still the same. The Matron walked into the room closing the door. I didn't recognise her.

"Can I help you?" She said, pulling the chair away from her desk. I thought she would offer me tuppence to buy some sweets.

"I used to stay here when my mum was in hospital, can I stay here for a while? I don't have anywhere to go. My husband was beating me. I left with the baby. I've been to the Homeless Families in Piccadilly."

"I must stop you there. I can't let you stay here. The home isn't run by the Jewish Community now, it belongs to the council. There is so much red tape. I'm sorry but I can't help you."

"Alright." I smiled at her.

I held onto the pushchair, it felt secure. Following her down the corridor, she opened the front door. I started walking towards the main road once again. Pausing for a moment near the bus stop, wondering whether or not to get the bus back into town, I knew the money I had wouldn't last very long and I needed it for food for us. I carried on walking. I stopped at a shop on the way to buy another bar of chocolate for the baby and a Mars bar for myself.

"I'll get you a hot drink when we get into town," I reassured him. He smiled back at me. I rang David's home. Anita answered the phone.

"It's Jane. Please can you help me? I've got a baby. My husband was hitting me. I've got nowhere to stay." There was a deadly silence.

"You've made your bed. Now lie in it." The phone slammed down.

It was getting dark when we got back to Piccadilly gardens. I noticed an all night café and went in. I sat the baby on my knee and helped him to drink his tea and ordered beans on toast for him. I remembered what the woman at the Homeless Families department had said, that if I was walking the streets with the baby I would be put into the police cells and the baby would be taken into care. I wondered if we would be able to stay in the café all night without being reported to the police. The baby's nappy needed changing so we had to go to the public toilets. Afterwards, I saw a bench in Piccadilly gardens. I sat down, before long I was falling asleep, still with one hand on the pushchair. The intense cold brought me back to reality. My mouth was parched, my body still aching from the beatings I had received. The baby was fast asleep. I looked around keeping my eyes peeled for any policemen walking about the gardens.

"What if they put me in the cells?" I whispered.

It was very dark, there was little activity on the streets. I grabbed the pushchair and headed once more for the all night café. It was nice and warm inside. I looked to see if there was a secluded seat so I could have a sleep. There wasn't. I ordered a cup of tea, a plate of chips and two slices of bread and butter. I was desperately cold and hungry. I lifted the baby out of his pushchair, placing him on my lap. He was still fast asleep. I stayed very still making sure my drink lasted as long as possible.

After a while I ordered another cup of tea. It was getting lighter outside. I wondered where I would go at daybreak. I watched people come and go, hoping they would keep the man behind the counter occupied so he wouldn't notice me. Soon the baby awoke and I bought another tea and egg on toast for his breakfast. People were on their way to work. It was time to leave the café. I changed the baby's nappy in the public toilets, still not knowing where I would go. I started on my way towards Cheetham Hill Road again. My head felt numb like ice as I walked, pushing the baby. This was the only part of Manchester I knew. On my way I noticed a phone box. I rang directory enquiries for the number of the Social Security office. I dialled the number and waited. The words shot out of my mouth in quick succession.

"I had to leave my husband with my baby because he was hitting me."

"What's your address?"

"I don't have one."

"We can't help you until you have an address."

"Alright, thank you." I smiled, replacing the receiver.

I walked and walked, in a trance. The landmarks that I dreaded didn't have any impact on me anymore as I walked past them. Not knowing what to do. Waiting at the bus stop at the top of Cheetham Hill Road, wondering if I should get the bus. There was nowhere to go. I looked to see if the 147 bus stop was still on Upper Park Road. It was still there. I carried on exhausted, hungry and cold not knowing what was happening. I wanted to curl up and sleep. On Upper Park Road I noticed a sign it read: *Bed and Breakfast*. I walked down the long path to the guest house, not knowing what I intended to do. I rang the front door bell, and waited, a middle aged lady appeared. She didn't say anything as I looked at her.

"Please, we haven't got anywhere to stay, my husband was hitting me." I opened the top buttons of my coat. "I'll clean for you." Tears were streaming down my face. "Please." I begged once more. The baby started crying. I leaned over to comfort him. "Please, just for a few days till I get a job and somewhere to live. I'll clean for you."

"Come in," the woman said. My body shook with relief.

"I'll start looking for a job tomorrow." I followed her down the hall. "Please can I go to sleep now? I'm very tired."

"You can have one of the attic rooms." I followed her up the stairs carrying the baby. She opened the door to the attic.

"Thank you." She closed the door behind her.

I pulled the covers back and laid the baby in the bed. I desperately wanted to feel warm. My mind and body were frozen to the bone. Holding onto him to feel his body heat, I curled up around him and slept. From time to time my eyes would open with a terrible sense of panic, thinking I was still back in the children's home waiting to go home to mum or in school not understanding anything that was being said or in the flat afraid I would be beaten. I held my breasts to comfort myself and slept.

CHAPTER 7

The following morning I heard a knock on the door. My body was still freezing cold and I didn't want to move out of the bed. "I won't be a minute." I switched the light on and off three times before opening the door. The woman was looking at me, not sure if she had done the right thing by taking me in. She walked into the room.

"What's your name?" she said, looking me up and down.

"Jane Levene." I cringed at the sound of it.

"You can stay here for a week or so, no more."

"That's alright. Thank you."

"You can do some cleaning jobs. These are for you."

She placed a carrier bag on the bed with some trousers, t-shirts and a cardigan. I watched as she closed the door. I knew she needed me. Later in the morning, I walked into town looking for a job. I wished I could buy myself some nice warm jumpers, my money was dwindling, I had to take care with it. Looking in shop windows to see if they were advertising for staff, there were no part-time vacancies. We had something to eat in a small café. The following day I would have to start looking in a different area of town.

Arriving back at the guest house, I looked for the woman to see if she wanted me to do any jobs. She told me she would like me to dust the lounge and that she had left us some food in the kitchen. I wondered if she had a daughter, then I realised that if she did she would be nice and clean.

"When I've done the jobs please can I go to my room and sleep?"

"Yes."

I took the baby with me to the lounge so I could keep an eye on him while I dusted. When all the work had been done I carried him to the room. We both slept till the following morning. We left the guest house and this time I started off in another direction. As I walked down the street, I noticed a small card in a sandwich shop window: *Urgently wanted, part-time sandwich maker.*

Walking through the door, my heart was pounding. I hoped there would be no need for written English or Maths, scales or punch card machines for making sandwiches. I prayed I would get the job. I was taken downstairs and told to knock on the office door.

"Are you the manager?

"That's what it says on the door."

"I've come about the job." I noticed him looking at the baby.

"Do you have someone to look after the baby?"

"Yes. I need a job. I'll work very hard." He paused for a while I could see he was thinking about it.

"Right, you can start tomorrow."

"Will I just be making sandwiches?"

"Yes."

Leaving the shop I started walking towards Cheetham Hill Road. "I've got a job." I told the baby, he had fallen asleep. Halfway up the road I heard a car horn. I didn't take any notice, the car stopped beside me, I looked through the window. It was David.

"Do you want a lift?"

"Yes please, I'm *oitskimatted.*" I folded the pushchair.

"I've just passed my driving test, this is Anita's car. If she finds out I've given you a lift, she won't let me use it again."

"I had to leave my husband. He was hitting me. This is my baby. Have you heard from Jeffery?"

"He's living in Bolton. He's married, living in a big house."

"What about dad, is he still alive?"

"I've heard rumours. People say things."

"What do they say?"

"Some say he's dead. Some say he's alive."

He dropped me off near the guest house. I thanked him for the lift, he drove off. I hurried back to tell the woman I had found myself a job. As I walked through the front door, she was walking down the hall. She looked around.

"I've got a job. I'll get the paper later. I need to get a flat for us." I smiled at her hoping she would be pleased with me. "I start the job tomorrow."

"Who's going to look after the baby?" She beckoned for me to follow her into the lounge and sat down.

"I don't know."

"I have to mention this. I've noticed a strong smell of urine in your room." I looked at her not understanding what she was saying. "I'll take care of him for a few days. Try to find somewhere to live."

"Thank you."

I folded the baby's pushchair and put it away. I did all the chores that needed doing. The baby woke me early in the morning. I looked at him. He was smiling and playing with the buttons on my coat. "I'm going to buy you nice toys when I get some money." I tickled his tummy. He smiled, I stroked his face and told him to *shloff* for a while. The job at the sandwich bar was from 11a.m. to 1p.m., so I would have time to look for a flat and do my work at the guest house. I was told to leave the baby in the lounge in his pushchair along with the nappies and food I had bought for him. I took enough money for my bus fare and left the house.

Walking down the drive, I stopped dead in my tracks, I couldn't feel my pulse. I stamped my foot on the ground to start it going again. Walking a little bit further stopping again, this time my heart felt as though it was being squeezed by a very strong hand. I felt light headed. I desperately tried to take a deep breath, it didn't work. I tried again, feeling very faint. I wished there was a wall to hold on to, afraid of dying and leaving the baby alone. If only I had the pushchair to hold onto. Dashing out of the grounds I soon found a wall I could stay close to and touch as I walked along. The sandwich shop was close to the bus stop. I felt relieved as I entered. Two women were busy making sandwiches.

"Take off your coat, I'll show you where to put it."

"I can't." My eyes focused on all the food.

"Why not?"

"I haven't got a jumper on."

"Yes, you have. I can see it." They looked at each other, saying nothing.

"Come over here. I'll show you what to do."

"Do I need to use scales?"

"No. Everything's either sliced or measured. Watch what I'm doing. Concentrate I'll only be showing you the once."

I could hear the two women chatting at the other side of the table. My thoughts were on the food. It was difficult to tear my eyes away from the food in front of me. The hunger was so powerful. I knew it would take all the horrible darkness from my head.

"Where do you live?" I lifted my gaze away from the food.

"Off Cheetham Hill Road. I'm looking for a flat."

"Well you haven't got a big Jewish nose. If you live in that area, you need one." They laughed.

"Are you married?"

"I've just left my husband."

"Do you have any children?"

"Yes, my baby, he's nearly two."

"You shouldn't have left your husband."

"He was hitting me."

"You shouldn't have left your husband if you have a baby. You must have asked for it."

I carried on making the sandwiches. "We're going for our break now."

I didn't take any notice, the smell of the food was too much. I looked up, they had gone. Picking up a slice of turkey breast, my heart started racing. My tummy was so desperately cold and empty, pushing the meat into my mouth, my hands were shaking. Frenziedly, I picked up five slices of bread and put them into my coat pocket, piling more meat into my mouth. Everything felt so much better now. I looked around once more to see if they were coming back. I pushed more bread and some cheese into my pockets.

The women arrived back. The man who had interviewed me was chatting to them. I could smell his body as he walked towards me. I moved away.

"Take off your coat and wear your overalls." I carried on making the sandwiches. I saw him glance over to the other women. "Clean your side of the table then you can go."

"I will. I promise."

Checking that all the food was in my pockets I made my way to the bus stop. I looked around to see if the evening newspaper was out.

When I arrived back at the guest house I thanked the women for looking after the baby. Putting him in his pushchair, I told him we were going for a walk. I found the nearest phone box. Looking through the directory, my heart was racing at the thought of speaking to Jeffery. My body ached with love. I wanted to look after him, to tell him I loved him and to stop him from feeling any hurt. I wished he would hurry and answer the phone, my tummy was aching so badly for some food.

"Hello?"

"Jeffery, it's Jane." My voice trembled. I'm in Manchester, I've left my husband he was hitting me."

"You want everything your own way. Just like mum." He put the phone down.

I found the nearest sweet shop and bought some chocolate and crisps. I passed a shop with a large front window. I grimaced at my reflection. It was so horrible.

The fire was on in the lounge when we arrived back. It looked so warm and inviting. "We'll go and get warm." The lounge was empty. I pushed the armchair towards the fire. I curled up on the chair holding the baby. He was smiling. I held his hand to see if he was getting warm. "I'll buy you lots of toys and nice things soon. You're such a good baby." My eyes started to close. The door creaked. The woman sat on the couch looking at me.

"I'm going to have to ask you to leave by Saturday."

"Alright." I smiled. I closed my eyes again and fell asleep.

I was in the school playground. I watched as a teacher approached me, wondering what I had done wrong. "Your mother's dying. She's been in that flat for years with no one to look after her." I looked at him. I didn't understand.

"I must get to her before she dies. I need her to know how much I love her. Why didn't anyone tell me she was living in the flat on her own?" I sobbed. He looked at me. I started running, desperately wanting to see her. "Mummy, mummy," I was repeating as I ran along the road.

I awoke with a jolt. "Wake up, wake up." The woman was shaking me.

The baby was crying and pulling at my coat. "We'll go and have a *shloff.*" I told the woman, carrying the baby towards the stairs. The dream lingered in my mind.

In the morning it was time for me to leave for work. I changed and fed him before sitting him in his pushchair in the lounge. Walking towards the bus stop my chest tightened. I felt faint. "What if I die before I get back to him? What if he thinks I've left him forever?" The words repeated in my head till it ached. I boarded the bus, closing my eyes when it passed my father's flat, the delicatessen, the Jewish Board of Guardians, the old doctor's surgery. They were all too painful to look at.

At work one of the women caught my eye. "Have you changed your clothes today? It doesn't look like you have."

"I'm going to get my stuff on Monday, some clothes and things." I looked at the list of sandwiches I had to make. My head lowered. Wanting them to leave me alone. Waiting for the women to take their break, I was desperately cold and hungry. They left the room and I stuffed as many pieces of meat, cheese and bread into my mouth as possible. Soon they returned.

"It's your break."

I headed for the toilet and stood near the wall. I pulled at my coat undoing the buttons, wanting to see my body, my huge tummy and breasts comforted me for a brief moment. I wanted rid of all the darkness, cold, hunger and isolation. I needed more food inside me. I knelt by the side of the toilet and forced my fingers down my throat. I began heaving. Feeling the food travelling up my throat towards my mouth, hardly digested, I needed to get every bit out so more could comfort me. I forced my fingers further down. I gagged heavily as my fingernails scratched the skin off the back of my throat. My eyes and nose streaming with water, my body became weak and heavy as I forced myself to vomit. I ached all over. Sitting down I forced the rest of the food down my throat. My heart racing, my head banging, I knew I must get back to work. I used the toilet for support and wiped my face.

"Finish your work, clear up then go."

"Alright."

After work I found the nearest phone box. I dialled David's number but there was no reply. Waiting for a few hours I tried again. Hoping Anita wouldn't answer the phone. I started dialling, my heart banging, I heard David's voice.

"It's Jane." I said in desperation, trembling from head to foot. Can I stay with you for a few nights? I have to move out of the guest house where I'm staying. I'm looking for a flat for us."

"I don't know. I told Anita I'd seen you and given you a lift, now she's refused to let me drive the car. It isn't a good idea."

I understood the silence. "Alright." I smiled, putting the receiver down. I could hear the baby crying. "Don't worry." I mimed, leaning over to kiss his forehead. I held on tightly to the pushchair handle and headed back towards the guest house.

"It's Thursday today, Friday tomorrow," I whispered, "It's Friday tomorrow, the food parcel from the soup kitchens." I could smell the aroma of the freshly baked bread, sitting on top of the little box of food with 'Levene' written on the side. I sniffed, my mind was steeped in the smell of the bread, stopping dead in my tracks and sniffing. There was a smell of burning in the air. I held on tighter to the pushchair. "It must be the guest house, it's burnt down." I told the baby, my heart pounding. My pulse had stopped working, stamping my foot lightly on the ground I felt faint but it worked, my heart was beating again. I carried on sniffing, looking around to see which way the wind was blowing. Wondering where we would go. Hurriedly I walked towards the large house. "Don't worry Hikey." I whispered repeatedly.

Walking around the corner my head aching, the smell of the smoke was still heavy. My heartbeat quickened, my chest tightened as I caught sight of the guest house. Sniffing again, there was no sign of fire I couldn't hear any fire engines. Perhaps the fire's in the cellar, maybe I should wait till the fire engines have been called. I could hear wood crackling, the smell of the smoke was overpowering.

"I'm not going to let you burn." I told the baby. Standing at the gate a couple walked past me. "Have you got the right time, please?" Watching carefully as the woman pulled back her coat sleeve.

"Twenty to five."

"Thank you." I said watching them walk into the distance. I waited for a while longer. "Have you got the right time, please?" I asked a young woman.

"It's five o'clock."

"Thank you." The baby was crying and stretching his arms towards me. "You must be hungry. The house isn't on fire. Don't worry." I whispered, stroking his hand.

The following morning I left for work. Outside the gate a woman was walking in my direction. "Have you got the right time, please?" At each corner I asked people the same question. Thanking them for taking the time to reply. At work one of the women beckoned me over to her side of the table.

"We're making different sandwiches now, here's your list." I looked at it.

"Does this mean I'm going to get the sack?"

"No." Looking at her friend I could hear them giggling as I walked back to my side of the table.

"Have you got the right time?"

"It's time you were working."

"Am I working tomorrow?"

"Yes. Why?"

I didn't reply. I wanted to be back at the guest house with the baby. In bed surrounded by piles of food so we wouldn't feel cold and hungry.

"What's your name?" a young man said, as he entered the kitchen.

"Jane." I replied without lifting my head. He started talking to the women, then turned to me.

"Where do you live?"

"In a guest house just off Cheetham Hill Road. I've got to be out by Sunday."

"Is your middle name Rebecca?"

"No." I heard giggling.

"That's good. Anyway, why are you living in a guest house?"

"I haven't got anywhere else to stay."

"You've got a baby."

"Yes."

"What about family?" I remained silent. "My ex-wife is looking for someone to share her house. Do you want me to ask her?"

"Yes. Please."

"I'll ring her now." He disappeared for a while. "She said it's OK. She lives in Ordsall. You can move in tomorrow. Have you got a lot of belongings?"

"No. I'm going to get some clothes, mum's candlesticks and photos on Monday."

"Here's Angie's address." He handed me a piece of paper.

After work I waited at the bus stop. "Have you got the right time, please?" I asked as I waited for the bus.

Sunday morning I collected my things, fed and changed the baby and made my journey to my new home in Ordsall. As I approached the house I looked at the baby. "She's a lovely lady. They told me at work." A tall woman with blonde frizzy hair and lots of makeup answered the door. Her stomach was so big I thought she was pregnant. She seemed a nice person and I was very relieved to have somewhere for the baby and I to live. "Is this the right house? Your husband said I could live here."

"Of course, come on in. Don't be shy. My name's Angie, he's my ex. I've heard all about you. Put your things in the corner, I'll put the kettle on."

I sat the baby on my knee. He was looking at me smiling. "I think we'll be OK now." I smiled at him.

"I'll make you a nice cup of tea and some biscuits. Take your coat off, make yourself at home."

"Can I leave it on please?"

"Tell me about your husband."

"I had to leave, he was hitting me. He wouldn't stop."

"You can stay here for as long as you pay your rent. I'll help you look after the baby during the day. You can pay me separately for that."

"I'm very tired. Can I go to bed?"

"It's only early. Why do you want to go to bed? Tell me about your family."

"My mum's dead. She died when I was 13, I think. I don't bother with my father. I don't like him."

"What about other family. There must be someone?"

"I have two brothers but, they don't..." I bowed my head.

"Don't what? What about granny or grandad?"

"They died before I was born."

"How old are you?"

"About twenty."

"Is something wrong with you? Why do you feel your wrist and neck? Steve said that sometimes you stamp your foot on the ground. Have you got 'St Vitas Dance' or something?"

"No. I just have to make sure my heart doesn't stop."

"Steve said you're a bit strange. Where's your family allowance book?"

"I'm going back to the flat on Monday to get it."

"Your handbag's a bit Aunt Twacky. What about Social Security?"

"I don't get that."

"Get to the Social Security office tomorrow. Pack in work. That's not going to pay you enough to stay here. Anyway Steve told me they're going to sack you."

"OK."

"Right. Let's sort out terms. You can pay me three pounds for your board. Two pounds for your food, there are extras. Your rent is due every Friday. You can have toast for your breakfast. I'll have your free milk and orange juice tokens. I don't want any cheek off you. I'm doing you a favour. No food in your room. I don't want mice."

"Can we go to bed now? We're very tired."

"I'll show you to your room."

CHAPTER 8

Monday morning, I started on my way to the flat to collect my belongings. I felt hungry and bought three Mars bars.

"Is this the bus to Liverpool?" I asked the bus conductor.

"Yes. That's what it says on the front."

"Please, will you tell me when we get there, please?"

"Liverpool is the last stop. You can't go any further."

My heart was pounding, I started sobbing when I turned the corner. The sight of the flat made me heave. I prayed Paul would be out at work. My neighbour passed me as I went through the main doors.

"What did you do to make him hit you?"

"Nothing."

"I'll bet. Young 'uns these days. Good for nothing."

I felt drowsy, wishing I could sleep for a long time. I walked up the stairs towards the flat fumbling in my pocket for the front door key. My hand felt numb as I turned the key in the lock. I pushed the front door open and shouted his name. There was no reply. Rushing to the living-room I picked up the candlesticks putting them in a carrier bag. The photos were in the sideboard. I looked around to see if there were any clothes for me and the baby. I picked up a few jumpers off the floor and put them on under my coat. It felt so good to feel their warmth. Hurriedly I rushed downstairs. The neighbour was at the bottom of the stairs.

"That poor baby! Only thinking of yourself," she said, tutting and nodding her head.

"Sorry." I lowered my head as I passed her.

"Women these days have no staying power!" she shouted. I remained silent relieved never to be going back.

It felt good to be on the bus going home. My eyes opened now and again, when the bus went over a bump or veered around a corner. I prayed I was on the right bus. Putting my hand inside my coat I held my breasts tightly and closed my eyes. "Don't worry Hikey. I love you." I whispered.

I collected my son and made my way to the Social Security office. It was a grey building, just like the one on Julia Street that I had visited with mum. There were rows of chairs all packed with people. There were so many different smells taking me back. My son was sitting in his pushchair. I stared at the floor and waited.

"Mrs Jones!" The sound of my married name startled me.

"Yes," I whispered. I was led into a room full of open-plan grey coloured cubicles. I sat down. A slight middle aged man with wavy black hair sat opposite. I didn't inhale.

"Do you have a permanent address?"

"Yes." I watched as he wrote my details on a form.

"You left your husband. Is that correct?"

"Yes."

"You'll have to get divorced, as soon as possible."

"OK."

"What was your maiden name?"

"Levene."

"That's a Jewish name isn't it?"

"Yes."

"Do your family help you financially?"

"No."

"Jews look after their own?" He looked at me.

"I don't know."

"What about your parents?

"I don't have any."

"Brothers, sisters?"

"I have a brother in Manchester."

"Does he help you?"

"No." I could hear other people being interviewed. I desperately wanted to go home and sleep.

"Speak up."

"No, he doesn't."

"Is he married?"

"No, he's adopted. He lives with Anita and Morris."

"Where do they live? I want to meet them. Tomorrow. I'll be there at nine o'clock."

I moved in my seat not sure what to do.

"That's all. You can go."

My heart racing, I went to the nearest phone box and rang David. "David I'm going to have to come round tomorrow. I've been to the Social Security and the man wants to meet me at your house."

"Why?"

"I think because he knows I'm Jewish."

"What's that got to do with anything?" There was a silence, then I could hear voices.

"David, I won't get any money. Please let me come."

"Anita isn't very happy about this. We don't seem to have any choice."

"I'm sorry." I put the phone down and held the pushchair as I walked home.

"Have you got the right time please?" I asked different people.

The following day I made my way to David's house. He opened the door. Anita was in the kitchen.

"Sit down, over there." David said.

My heart pounded as I heard Anita banging about in the kitchen. I caught a glimpse of her and lowered my eyes.

"Nobody's going to want you now you've got a baby. No man wants a loaf that's been half-eaten. No nice *Yiddishy* man is ever going to want you. You made your bed, you lie in it. I'm not very happy about being dragged into this. What will the neighbours think? We've never been *shnorrers*. Have we, Morris?"

Morris was reading the newspaper. He didn't lift his head his cigarette smoke rising to the ceiling.

"Well where is he?" she shouted, looking through the curtains, "I hope the neighbours don't notice him."

"Sorry Anita. He'll be here in a minute."

The baby started crying. Anita walked over and looked at him. "Poor little thing. What chance is he going to have in life?"

I saw the man from the Social Security walking up the path. "He's here, David."

Anita opened the door. She ushered him in quickly. He turned to David.

"Are you the brother?"

"Yes."

"I need to know if you support your sister financially."

"No."

"Are you aware of any financial support from other family members or Jewish organisations?"

"No."

The officer looked at me. "Sign this undertaking." He laid a document on the table checking through it. "You'll get your book in the post within the next few days. Have you got your Family Allowance book?"

"No."

"Where is it?"

"I left it in the flat when I left my husband."

After he left Anita lifted the baby out of his pushchair. "What a lovely little boy." She sat him on her lap, looking at me. "You're so irresponsible, just like your mother. I always said to Morris and David, it won't be long before she gets pregnant. David didn't even know how to eat a meal at the table when we first got him. He was dragged up. We wouldn't dream of eating our meals on the floor. Go and make us a cup of tea. It's the least you can do."

"OK." I lifted my gaze slightly, my head felt very heavy. I felt desperate to eat. Morris carried on reading the newspaper, dragging on his cigarette. David sat watching the television.

"What's that smell! What the hell are you doing?!" Anita stormed into the kitchen.

"Making cups of tea," I replied. She pulled me back away from the stove lifting the kettle.

"That's an electric kettle. You don't put it on the stove you plug it in! You've ruined it. Are you mad or simply careless?"

I didn't understand what I had done wrong.

During the week my Social Security and Family Allowance books arrived.

"There's post for you. It's your books. I'll keep them safe. Come on, we'll go to the Post Office. I want your orange juice and milk vouchers" Angie shouted.

We got back to the house. She gave me some spending money and kept the rest.

"I've got plans for *you*."

"What for?"

"I've got a friend coming round tonight. I'd like you to meet him. Very nice he is. I'll lend you one of my shirt dresses. It's cream, sort of 'crepey' very smart. Keep the top buttons open. I don't want you looking like Aunt Twacky when he arrives. I want you to have a bath, wash your hair. I want you all spruced up. Are you listening? You seem a little lacking in that department, a bit manky if you don't mind me saying so. Rob's going to be here by eight."

"I'm very tired and cold. I want to go to bed."

"You're very ungrateful. I've arranged a welcoming party for you. All you can do is moan. I don't think we're going to get on."

"I'm sorry."

"I think you should find somewhere else to live."

"I'm sorry. Honest. Please let me stay."

"Are you going to have one drink with us or not?"

"OK." I slept till the evening in bed with the baby.

"Jane, get down here. Rob's pulled up. Come on now. Put your friendly face on. Do you hear?"

"Yes. OK." I put the dress on she had left on the bed. Angie was sitting on the couch with Rob. I looked away when I caught smell of his body.

"Come on, Jane sit on the other side of Rob. Us blondes have more fun, *don't* we Jane? I'll get you a drink of red wine."

"I don't like red wine."

"What do you drink?"

"Pop."

"Oh she's a laugh isn't she? We don't want Rob to think you're not a woman of the world do we? Drink this red wine Jane. You know you like it."

"What the hell's she doing? Banging her foot on the floor?"

"I'm starting my heart."

"Jane, *shut* your gob. Drink that fucking wine. Take no notice of her, she's got a weird sense of humour. Not bad looking though, is she Rob?"

"No. Not bad at all."

"Doesn't she look pretty in that dress, Rob? It's one of mine, doesn't quite look as good as on me. She's got nice legs. Pull your skirt up and let Rob see them."

"Do you fuck around?" he asked, "have you got any sisters? Invite them to our party." Rob said. I looked at the floor.

"I haven't got any sisters. I'm going to have to go to bed. I'm very tired."

"Listen, stupid. You're going nowhere, stay put and talk to Rob. He's come all the way from South Manchester to see you. You like Steve my ex, don't you? Anything in trousers, eh!"

"I'm very tired." I went upstairs to the bedroom. I could hear heated conversation downstairs. The baby was sleeping. I heard footsteps on the stairs. The door flew open.

"Jane, before you go to sleep, Rob wants to have a word."

"I've had enough of this. Get out of my way, Angie. This one's definitely on for tonight." He pulled back the blankets lunging at the bed. I was wearing knickers and a jumper. "I like the look of this." Before I had chance to move he was on top of me pinning me down. I lay still, frozen in time in fear of my life. He got off me and rushed out of the room. I could hear them talking.

"She's frigid. I want my money back."

"Look Rob. Leave it a few weeks. Give her chance to settle in. Let's see what happens."

I heard them both run down the stairs. They were shouting at each other. I cuddled the baby, pulling the sheets over us. The door pushed open.

"You little *bitch*. You're a prick tease aren't you? You could have showed him you were enjoying it. Did you enjoy making an arse of me like that? Your rent's going up. Don't touch any of my food. Are you listening, bitch?"

"Yes."

One morning I woke up, there was a man standing in the room. His name was Jim she had taken money off him. I knew he was lonely and needed me. I couldn't bear the thought of hurting him. I smiled as he pulled the blankets back.

"You enjoy your work?"

I looked at him not understanding what he meant. I knew he needed me that was all that mattered. I held him, kissing him.

"You're a fucking good shag." He got dressed. "I'll definately be back to see you."

I heard the front door slam and ran to the window. I watched as he walked down the street, knowing he would feel good now that he had someone to care for him. Like the other men who came.

Every day I bought an evening paper. Usually the adverts for flats to rent read: *no children*, but one day I noticed an attic flat. I rang and made an appointment to view it in the evening. They didn't mind that I had a toddler. The house was on Bolton Road, it was a large run down property. I pushed the front door open, the lock was loose. It was dark and gloomy inside. The smell of damp filled the air. I walked up the bare stairs till I reached the attic. Queuing behind five other people waiting to view it, in turn each person was shown around the bedsit. In turn they each refused it. When it was my turn a middle aged woman hurried me into the room. The door to the room was hanging off its hinges and the walls were clearly very damp. There was a single bed behind a two-seater sofa, an old chest of drawers and threadbare rug. The only window was a small attic window.

"It's yours if you want it. The toilet and bathroom are downstairs. That's where you get your water. It's a slot meter for the bath. The electric meter's behind you.

"Yes. I'll have it. Can I move in tomorrow? Please."

"Yes. No pets. No men. This is a respectable house."

I got back to Angie's house. She wasn't in. I went to bed and waited till I heard the front door slam. "Angie." I shouted at the top of the stairs. "I'm moving out tomorrow. I need my Social Security books." My heart was pounding, my chest tight. I knew I was hurting her. She needed me. Just like the men she had brought to see me. How would I ever forgive myself? My legs were trembling so much it was difficult to walk.

"Jane, don't be silly. You know how much I love having you here. I don't know what I'll do if you leave. I saw Jim the other day. I gave him a right bollocking for getting hot under the collar. You're an attractive little thing. I can't help it if men lose control when they see you. You know what men are like, don't you?"

"I could smell his socks."

"Silly you, he told me he'd like to take you out for a meal somewhere, just you and him. He can be very generous you know. I have a lot of male friends like him, very generous. They would like to meet you. You do look attractive when you have a bit of makeup on. I'm sure we can tart you up again."

"But my brother wants me to go and live with him. I can't hurt his feelings."

"Little bitch. I was going to give you notice anyway. My boyfriend's moving in soon."

"I don't want to hurt your feelings. I know you need me." I cried.

"I think you've got some sort of sickness or something. The way you sit, staring into space banging your foot on the floor. You're round the bend. That's what I think."

I sat watching her.

"God help your brother, that's all I can say."

I arrived at the flat on Bolton Road with my few possessions, the baby in his pushchair, the landlady was waiting for me.

"Are there any blankets?"

"No, you provide your own. I provide the flat, you provide blankets, pots and pans. Get in touch with the Social Security for a voucher. I'm doing you a favour not charging you a month in advance. She left the room. I was so tired I could hardly keep awake.

"I'm going to make you some nice chicken soup soon." I smiled at the baby. I looked at the 'Baby Belling' the wall was very damp, the socket hung loose. We lay on the bed and both fell asleep.

The following morning waking up I felt itchy, scratching all over. I was covered with red spots. I looked at the baby he had spots on him too. I straightened myself and the baby and went downstairs. When I opened the front door my legs immediately turned to jelly. I seemed so small and lightweight, I felt that the wind would blow me away. I held the door frame to stop myself from fainting. I had seen a chemist shop on my

way to view the flat it was on the same block. I rushed there
and showed the chemist the spots.

"They're bed bug bites. I have a spray. Use it on the mattress
and dab the calamine lotion on the spots." I looked in my
handbag.

"I haven't got enough money for the calamine lotion. I
need to buy some food."

"Do you want the spray?"

"Yes please." On the way back to the flat, I bought some
cheese and bread, enough for today and tomorrow. I sprayed
the mattress and the bed then laid the baby next to me on the
couch. We fell asleep. I didn't have the energy to stay awake
or attempt to do anything. There was nowhere to put the food
so I left the remains on top of the Baby Belling. In the morning
when I went to get the food. It had been mostly eaten. The
cheese had large teeth marks in it. I fell asleep again. The
following day I rang my brother.

"Hello?"

"It's Jane. Sorry to bother you, Jeffery."

"What do you want? I'm busy."

"Please can I come and see you with the baby? I'm living
on Bolton Road now. I've got an attic flat. Please can I come
and see you?"

"No. I don't want my wife's family to know I have a sister
who's a one parent family. The trouble with you you're always
feeling sorry for yourself. I don't want you here. I've just paid
a thousand pounds for my mother-in-law to have an
operation."

"OK Jeffrey. Bye."

I got into bed with the baby. As soon as I closed my eyes I
dreamt that my mother was still alive, one of the nightmares

that haunted me most of the time. I awoke with a jolt and watched as a rat ran over the bed. I held the baby close to me.

The landlady called to collect the rent.

"Have you got the rent?"

"Yes. There's mice and rats in the flat."

"It's pigeons. You can hear them on the roof." She looked very angry. My heart started banging.

"I've seen them. They eat my food. One ran over the bed last night."

"You're mistaken. If you mention this to anyone I'll send my son around to sort you out. He won't hesitate and I have to warn you he's a big lad. He'll put you out onto the street. Most landladies won't take children. You don't know when you're well off."

"Sorry." I said. My body shaking from head to foot. I heard her slam the front door. "We'll make a nice bed for you." I told the baby as I pulled out the bottom drawer from the large chest. I tore a piece of blanket and made a bed for him. "This is where you'll sleep. Mummy loves you."

The following week I was going to the shops around the corner for some food. I noticed a woman approaching me.

"Is your name Jane?"

"Yes, have I done something wrong?"

"There's a young man, he's been showing your photo to people asking if they've seen you. I think he knows where you live."

"Oh!" Straight away, I knew it must be Paul. "What does he look like?"

"He's tall with short fair hair. He said he's your husband."

My heart started pounding, my lungs emptied of air. I rushed to the Post Office, I gasped for air to see if I could start my lungs working again. I felt my heart, it was still pounding. After collecting my money I hurried back to the flat, knowing that I couldn't lock myself in because the flat door was still off its hinges. Pushing the baby, I started sobbing. Praying he wouldn't find the house where I lived or maybe get tired of looking and go home. The front door was slightly open. It was easy to open because the door frame was rotten. I took the baby out of the pushchair and carried him up the stairs. I turned the corner and climbed the last few stairs. My head was pulled back with such force I dropped the baby.

"I want you to come home."

"No."

It was difficult to speak as he punched me repeatedly. He pushed me to the floor and started kicking me. The baby was crying.

"I need you. You're coming back with me. Get the baby."

"How did you find me?" I sobbed.

"Jeffery told me you lived on Bolton Road."

"I don't want to come back with you." I stayed still acting dead, praying for the nightmare to end. He carried on shouting and hitting. I remained on the floor, refusing to leave. I closed my eyes. I could hear Paul crying.

"I love you. Please come home with me."

I closed my eyes as he lunged towards me once more pulling at my hair, shaking my body. I said nothing. I heard his footsteps descending the stairs. I got on the bed with the baby beside me, covering us both with the blankets. When I heard the front door slam, I got up and combed my hair.

CHAPTER 9

We had been living in the flat for about three months. Each day I walked my son to school, then walked down the road to the sweet shop, bought chocolates and crisps, then slept until it was time to collect him from school. I waited in the playground. One of the teachers came over to me. I looked at her.

"He smells of urine."

"Oh." I reached for his hand, smiling at him.

"It was very noticeable in class."

"OK." Starting to walk towards the school gate, she followed me.

"You're missing the point. You must do something about it."

"Alright."

"You're my son, not hers. She's only pretending to be nice and clean." I knew how false she was, how much she liked pretending. We headed back towards the flat. In the path, I noticed a few bricks and two small planks of wood. I pushed the front door open and told my son to wait in the hall. I picked up the bricks and put the planks under my arm. "I'm going to make a bookshelf for us. I'll buy you some books when I have the money," I smiled at him. There were four bricks. I placed them near to the wall and put the planks across them making two shelves.

"Come on. Mummy's going to buy you a present."

"What, Mummy? A moto car?"

"No." I held his hand, remembering where the second-hand shop was. "We'll go and buy some books to put on the shelf." I noticed an illustrated history book. It had pictures of different people on the front. I couldn't look inside. I hated myself when I picked it up.

"Mummy, read me a story."

"No. We'll look at the pictures. I'll buy you a book each time I get my money. One with lots of pictures." We walked back to the flat. I sat him on the bed and gave him the book to look at.

"Look, Mummy!"

"No, you read it." I couldn't open it or read it. I finished some chocolate that was in my handbag. The thirst for food was desperate. "Mummy's going to the loo. I won't be long. You look at the book." I hurried down the stairs. "I hate you, I hate you, I hate you." My heart started pounding as I closed the toilet door. My fingers down my throat, my head aching. I struggled to heave. I saw myself in the mirror. It was my mother's face. "Mummy, mummy." As I heaved I felt wet down my legs. Suddenly, I felt comforted. I looked in the toilet, I had got rid of most of the chocolate. I felt very weak and crawled back up the stairs.

"Mummy, what's this?" He pointed at the book.

"I don't know. Mummy having a *shloff* now. Be a good boy." I slept for a few hours. When I awoke my son was laying beside me. I got up and tried to make the bookcase look nice.

"Who's that?" He asked as I placed the photograph of my mother on the shelf alongside the candlesticks.

"It's my mummy, these candlesticks belonged to her." He walked over and looked at the photograph of her.

"Where's your mummy now?"

"In hospital." My heart sank.

"We going to see her?"

"No."

"She'll be on her own." He cried, tears streaming down his face. "I want to see her." He said pulling at my coat.

"She's dead." I cuddled him. He was still crying. "Look at the book I bought for you. These pictures are nice." I sat on the floor beside him watching while he opened it again. "I'll buy you lots of nice books when I get some money."

Soon he stopped crying, becoming engrossed in the book, looking at the pictures and spelling the words. I took his hand.

"I need to go to the phone, come on."

I carried him down the stairs. He kept hold of his book. I rang David's number and Anita answered the phone.

"Can I speak to David please? It's Jane." I begged.

"What for?"

"I'd like to meet him in town and buy him something to eat. Please." I said.

"He's busy."

"Alright. Thank you," I replied. The line was already dead.

"Come on, we'll go to *shloff*. When we get a nice gas stove, I'm going to make you nice meals" I was telling him as I lay on the bed.

Leaving my son in the school playground I started walking in the direction of a solicitors office.

"Have you got the right time please?" I enquired as a young woman passed me.

The receptionist made an appointment for me to see the solicitor the following week. I told the solicitor what had happened with Paul. I had to sign an affidavit. Then wait for the court date.

The day arrived. I met the solicitor outside the court. She told me that my husband would not be contesting the case. I waited in the corridor until my name was called. Then, directed to the witness stand, I stood with my head bowed. The court was full of people. I was asked to confirm my name and address.

"What religion are you?"

"Jewish," I said my head bowed.

"You will have to speak up."

"Jewish."

"I want you to explain in your own words why you are seeking a divorce."

"My husband hit and kicked me every day. I don't know what I did wrong. He put a pillow over my face and tried to suffocate me. He wouldn't let me use the fire or hair dryer and then I got bronchial pneumonia when I was pregnant. They took me into hospital." I still had my head bowed and wished it was all over. I explained more of why I had left. I looked up, the people in the gallery were watching me. They knew I was to blame. I lowered my head again. There was deadly silence.

"Miss Levene, please look at me," the Judge said. "Well, we can't expect this nice young lady to live under circumstances like that, divorce granted."

The door to the flat was still off its hinges, leaning against the wall. The walls still too damp to plug in the Baby Belling cooker and there was nowhere to put any food. When I could afford it I bought food from the Chinese takeaway around the corner. That was the only hot food we ate.

Weeks passed. One morning, I went back to bed after taking my son to school. I was woken by heavy footsteps on the stairs.

"Jane. It's David, Anita is with me. Wake up."

"Hello, David." I smiled.

"We've brought you some food." He handed me a small box. "We need to talk to you."

"What's the matter?"

"Anita and Morris have a friend. His name's Ivan. He escaped the concentration camps when he was a boy. He lost all his family. He's got money. He gets a good pension. You won't go short of anything. He's got a nice car." I looked at him.

Anita entered the room. "You need to marry him." She said. I cringed.

She looked at me. "Do you like living like this? He can give you everything you need to look after the baby. He's outside. Tidy yourself. David, go and get him." I couldn't say no. My heart was racing, I knew I would smell his body if he came upstairs. I could hear Anita's voice.

"Jane. This is Ivan."

I looked. He was a middle aged man, very large, he looked like Morris.

"We'll go downstairs wait in the car. You and Ivan get to know each other."

My whole body was trembling as I heard the footsteps going down the stairs fading into the distance. I could smell his body.

"Come, sit next to me." I sat on the bed, saying nothing. I saw him lunge towards me.

"You're an attractive woman. Come here, I want to kiss you." I ran over to the tiny window, he followed me. "I'll catch you," he said, as he grabbed my arm. "I want to kiss you."

He pushed me against the wall. I couldn't breathe, I got away and ran down the stairs, out of the front door. They were sat in the car. Looking at me, I could see Anita frowning.

"Where's Ivan?"

"I'm here, Anita. What's wrong with her?"

"Why? What did she do?" Anita asked.

"Nothing, didn't want to talk. Ran away like a *meshugginah*."

"I wash my hands of her. Get in the car, Ivan. We'll go home. She made her bed, she can lie in it."

I heard Anita's voice as the car drove off. I didn't want them to go. I ran into the house and looked out of the window before getting into bed, I was shaking. I pulled the blankets over myself "Go to *shloff* Hikey." I whispered, holding my breasts for comfort. I was nice and warm, soon I fell asleep.

After I picked my son up from school, I rang David. Anita was out.

"Why couldn't you marry him? Like Anita said he could have given you everything. Don't you wish you could live in a big house like Jeffery?"

I went back to the flat.

Summer arrived. I collected my son from school. It was a hot sunny day. As we headed back towards the flat I noticed people wearing their summer clothes, chatting to each other. We walked up the path to the house.

"Let's sit on the step."

"It's sunny, Mummy. Can we go for a walk?

"Yes. After mummy's had a *shloff*." I knew I couldn't do it; the brightness of the sun made me feel very sad. I didn't like it. I needed to be indoors. We went upstairs and slept. Noises woke me. As I opened my eyes, a rat ran over me. I could hear more of them scurrying around the room. I looked at my son in bed. I hadn't been able to get out to the shops. I remembered what the teacher had said about him smelling. Not knowing what to do to help him. Feeling desperate I went down to the bathroom to force myself to vomit. I noticed someone had left a bottle of tablets on the side of the bath. I picked them up, not knowing what they were or caring. Opening the bottle I poured them into my hand. Putting four into my mouth then taking the rest out of the bottle I swallowed them. The sound of my son's voice shouting me brought me back to reality. I didn't want to die and leave him without a mother. Putting my fingers down my throat I tried to vomit. I ran up the stairs stamping my feet on the ground hoping it would stop the tablets from killing me.

"Come on. We need to go out." Rushing to the doctor's surgery around the corner, I begged to see the doctor. "I've taken some pills. Please let me see the doctor." The receptionist disappeared.

"How many have you taken?" she asked, when she returned.

"About eight, I made myself sick." I watched as she knocked on the doctor's room once more.

"Sit down. The doctor will be about five minutes." I waited, holding my son close to me.

"What's wrong, Mummy?"

"Nothing."

"Why are you crying?"

"I'm not." I sat him on my knee. "Mummy loves you."

"The doctor will see you now." It was a young female doctor. "Sit down."

"How many tablets did you take?"

"Eight. I made myself sick."

"Why did you take them?"

"I don't know." I couldn't stop coughing.

My son was also coughing badly. She examined us both.

"You've got bronchitis and a throat infection. I'll give you some antibiotics. I'm going to refer your son to Hope Hospital because of his severe cough."

"OK."

She looked at my neck.

"That's a nasty rash. Have you been scratching it? It's seeping. Take your jumper off." I was wearing two t-shirts and two jumpers.

She noticed my chest and arms were also covered in a rash.

"I'll give you some cream for that, you mustn't scratch it or it will spread. Are you neglecting yourself?"

"No."

"Do you have any family?"

"No."

"What do you do with your day?"

"Sleep."

"It sounds to me like you're sleeping because you can't face life."

"Don't know." I replied, not understanding what she meant.

We got back to the flat. I got into bed with my son. I had the antibiotics at the side of the bed. I closed my eyes and poured them into my hand. Swallowing a handful of them with a glass of water I relaxed in the bed. I slept for a while. Waking up my heart was pounding, my son tucked into me. After a while I rushed around to the surgery again, pleading with the receptionist to see the doctor because I didn't want to die.

"Did you intend to overdose?" the doctor asked.

"Yes. I think. I don't know."

"Why?"

"I don't know."

"I can arrange for you to see a psychologist. He holds group counselling sessions on Wednesday evenings in one of the houses across the road. I strongly suggest you go along."

"OK," I replied.

"I'll refer you. You'll get confirmation in the post."

The following Monday morning I left my son in the school playground. "When we get a stove, I'm going to make you a nice party for us." I kissed him and watched as he rushed into school.

I collected my money from the Post Office. On the way back I noticed a hardware shop. I wanted utensils so I could prepare some chopped and fried fish.

"How much is the *ribizon* and do you have a *hackmesher*?"

"What?"

"A *hackmesher* and a *ribizon* you have in the window. When I get a stove I want to make some chopped and fried fish for us."

"I'm sorry. I don't know what you're talking about."

Some days later when I collected my son from school. He was crying, telling me he didn't feel well. His chest problems had worsened.

"Let's go and ring Jeffery." My heart pounded as I approached the phone box. His wife answered the phone. "It's Jane. Can I come and see you?"

There was silence. I could hear voices and shouting. I put the phone down. I looked in the phone book and got his address. The bus for Bolton came.

"Come on. We'll go and see Jeffery."

I arrived in Bolton. It was cold, damp and dark. My son was listless in my arms. "We'll see Jeffery soon." I knocked on the front door.

"You'd better come in." I sat on the couch with my son on my lap. There was an uncomfortable silence.

"Are you hungry?" his wife asked.

"Yes. Very."

"Will you have some stew?"

"Yes, please." I looked at Jeffery. He went over to his record player and put on a record of sound effects.

"You'll enjoy this." He said, turning the volume so that the sound vibrated around the room. My son started crying.

"Here. Give him to me. Has he wet himself? He smells," his wife said.

"Don't know," I said, as I ate the stew. "Jeffery, look I've got a Post Office book. I've got a few pounds, I'm putting it away tomorrow. I'm going to get a job so we can have a nice carpet."

"What are you showing me for? Are you trying to make me jealous?"

I ate my stew in silence, my son crying from time to time.

"What time are you going?" Jeffery asked.

"I don't know when the last bus is due. It's foggy out there. Will you take me to the bus station? Please."

Jeffery and his wife looked at each other.

"I'll take you now. The last bus is about ten o'clock."

The bus station seemed empty. I watched as he drove off. "Bye Jeffery." I said under my breath.

"What time's the last bus to Manchester?" I asked someone in the bus station office.

"It's gone."

It was getting colder. My son was shivering. I opened the phone box door and lifted the phone.

"Jeffery."

"What do you want?"

"I've missed the last bus. Please will you take us home? He's not well."

The phone slammed. I wasn't sure what to do so I waited. Soon I saw Jeffery's car pull up near the station.

"Are you giving me a lift?"

"Get in. I'm not happy about this."

I sat in the back with my son. The car was going so fast I cried out. "Please don't go so fast."

"If you don't shut it you can get out and walk. OK?"

"OK, Jeffery." I was relieved when the car stopped outside the flat.

"Do you know how much that would have cost in a taxi?"

"No, Jeff."

"Give me the five pounds you've got. I haven't got any change but if I see you again I'll give you another lift."

"OK, Jeffery." I smiled. I watched as he drove into the distance.

I was glad to be back in the flat. It was so cold. We got into bed. The following morning I took my son to the doctor. He had chicken pox.

The referral arrived to see the psychologist. I had no idea what a psychologist was or what would happen. Arriving at his consulting room I waited.

"Miss Levene."

"Yes." I said frowning. I followed him into his room, lowering my head.

"I would like you to do something for me." I raised my head slightly, watching as he took a mirror out from a drawer in the desk.

"What do you see when you look in the mirror?" He held it in front of my face. My body tensed, instinctively my face screwed up, I glanced quickly in the mirror.

"A big nose, holes all over my face. It's horrible." I said pulling away, my head lowered.

"Well, I see an attractive face." The words didn't penetrate my thinking.

"What do you see when you see your reflection?"

"My mum."

"What do you mean when you say, your mum?"

"I feel like my mum,"

"What about Jane."

"Don't know." I frowned at the mention of my name.

"Would you like to attend the weekly group meetings?"

"Yes, please."

The following week I left the flat and made my way to see the psychologist. Walking towards the house I dreaded the thought of being in a room with other people.

"Have you got the right time. Please?" I asked people on the way there.

Soon the house was in sight. My heart pounding I waited at the front gate not sure what to do. People were arriving. I asked the time from each person that passed me, watching as they walked in and up the stairs. Feeling faint at the thought of being in a room with all those people, I summoned up the energy to go in. Walking up the stairs, engulfed in all the old atmospheres I knew. I walked down the corridor, I could see people arranging chairs around the room. I pulled a chair over and sat near the door. The psychologist sat down.

"Jane, do you realise that you asked each person in here, the time, before you entered the building."

I held my lips tightly closed lowering my head more. I knew I had done something wrong.

"Why are you holding your lips closed? This is therapy. You need to talk."

He didn't understand that I would get into trouble if I opened my big mouth. One of the people came over to me. My head ached.

"Come and sit with the group?" I hesitated.

"Oh let her *sit* there if she wants," one of the other group members said. I smiled at him.

"Someone shows you kindness and you reject them. Another rejects you and you smile. You seem to understand rejection but not kindness. You have things the wrong way round," the psychologist said.

"I don't know." I said, rising from my seat and running out of the room. "I don't like any of them." I whispered as I headed towards the flat. Pushing the front door open I rushed up the stairs desperate to eat the chocolate I had bought from the shop.

"Hello." I heard a voice from the landing below.

"My name's Jenny, this is my little girl Sam. What's your name?"

"Jane."

"Why haven't you got a door on your flat? If I were you I'd get the landlady to fix that. It's disgusting. Come down and have a cup of tea with me sometime."

I got into bed, ate my chocolate and went to sleep. Later that evening I was woken. I could hear banging, it seemed to be coming from Jenny's flat. I looked onto the small landing, a man came out of her flat. I quickly got back into bed. I could hear footsteps.

"Jane, my boyfriend's doing some work in the flat. He's building a bunk bed for Sam, he won't be long."

"OK."

"Come and have a drink with us, he's got a bottle of red wine."

"No, thanks." I put my head under the blankets and fell asleep. The following night I heard Jenny's door open. I could hear footsteps.

"Jane. I have to go to work. I've left Sam in bed. Will you listen out for her, if she cries go in and see if she needs anything, I've left the door open."

"Alright," I fell asleep.

I was back in the room with the psychologist and the others at the meeting. It looked and smelt like the living-room at Bracknell Court. The psychologist was lying on the couch. He had blood on his legs. My mothers handbag was on the floor beside him. Each person in turn had sex with him on the couch. It was my turn. He asked me for money. "Why have I got to pay? Why didn't you ask the others for money?"

"Jane, Jane. Are you OK? You're shouting."

I awoke with a jolt, trembling. "What time is it?"

"Three in the morning." Jenny was standing near the bed. "I had my door closed and I could hear you shouting."

"He had sex with everyone, then when it was my turn he charged me."

"You were dreaming. You're talking like it was real. Why have you got all your clothes on? I couldn't sleep like that, I'd be uncomfortable."

"No. I'm fine."

"It's really good, this job. With the extra cash I earn I'm going to save for a deposit on a decent flat. Should have enough money to have it how I want. They're looking for a glass collector. Why don't you apply?"

"OK. I want to buy some carpet."

"Leave it with me. I'll speak to the manager tomorrow night. Will you listen out for Sam again?"

"Yes."

The following morning I took my son to school, bought some food, got into bed and fell asleep. I was woken by footsteps on the stairs. I could hear two women talking. The steps were getting closer. They stopped. They were banging on Jenny's door. I stayed very still.

"Jenny, open the door. It's your Social Worker. I need to talk to you urgently." I heard the door creak open.

"What's the problem?" Jenny asked.

"The problem is your three year old daughter has vaginal bleeding, again! Where do you keep your contraceptive pills?" The door closed. I heard voices again. More footsteps.

"Jane, I need to speak to you." Jenny was standing by the broken door. "I can do without this. I hate being stuck in the flat with a kid. It's driving me mad. I'm looking for another flat. I'd live with my mother but all she can say is, I told you so. Should have listened to her and gone on the pill sooner." She sat on the bed. "It's not my fault if the kid gets hold of my pills when I'm not looking. If it happens again they'll take her into care. I'm going to make a coffee. Do you want one?"

"No thanks, I'm very tired." I pulled the blankets over my head.

The glass collecting job was in a nightclub. I rang and arranged to go and see the manager.

"We're looking for barmaids."

"I can't do that."

"Why?"

"I don't know how to add up."

"You'll pick it quickly, I'm sure." He went behind his desk and passed me a small clear plastic bag with a pair of black tights in it."

"I don't wear black tights."

"They're not tights. That's your uniform."

I pulled it out of the bag. It was like a tiny swimming costume. "Please don't make me wear that. Please can I collect glasses?"

"Fine. Start tomorrow night." I could see he was angry. I knew I had upset him.

On my first night it was difficult to stay awake. It was very hot walking around the club wearing my coat. Noticing two young women that I recognised from school, I lifted my head. Trying to raise a smile and make eye contact, they looked me up and down. They quickly turned, walking away.

I couldn't wait to get into bed when I arrived back at the flat. My son was sleeping, I hugged him and felt my eyes closing.

In the morning I took my son to school. As I walked the short distance back to the flat, I stopped and asked a young man the time.

"Hey, you asked me that yesterday. What's your name?"

"Jane."

"Where are you going?"

"Home, after I've bought some food."

"Come on I'll buy us some fish and chips. I work in the office next to the school. Are you married?"

"No."

"Do you have a boyfriend?"

"No."

"Come on, we'll take the fish and chips back to your place."
I sat on the corner of the couch and he sat on the bed.

"Are you on the pill?"

"No."

"Go to the doctor tomorrow and get some. I'm going now. I'm away for a few days. I'll see you next week. Don't forget, the doctors tomorrow."

I watched as he left the flat. Running to the tiny window, I watched as he walked onto the car park of the office next door. I got into bed and slept.

Returning from school the following day I noticed a van outside the house. It was Jenny's boyfriend.

"She's moved out," he told me.

My heart sank. I pushed the front door and it creaked open. The door to the room on the left opened. A slight, attractive woman with black curly hair opened the door. She looked like Minnie Shelefski.

"Do you live here?"

"Yes, in the attic."

"I had to leave my husband. He was a violent bastard. Won't be staying here long, no more than a few weeks, it's a shit-hole."

I felt extremely tired going up the stairs. I stopped at the bathroom to make myself sick. When I had finished, my head was pulsating, my face red and hot, liquid pouring from my eyes and nose. I crawled up the remaining stairs to the attic. I got into bed too tired to keep my eyes open.

My heart ached. I wondered how Auntie Doris was. Perhaps she was ill and needed me. I thought about Jeffery and David. I looked across the road at the bus stop. Should I go and see Auntie Doris? I crossed the road. My legs felt like jelly. My lungs were failing. Feeling faint I waited for the bus. "Do you have the right time?" I asked people waiting at the bus stop. "I'll buy some chocolate for Auntie Doris." I whispered. I looked into the distance to see if there was a bus coming. I held onto the bus shelter, feeling dizzy, unreal. I knew my heart wasn't big or strong enough to pump the blood around my body.

"Here's the bus." I heard someone say.

"Is it going into town?" I asked the person standing next to me.

The bus stopped. Stepping onto the platform, holding the pole for support I asked the conductor if it was going into town.

"Yes."

"Will you let me know when we get there?"

The bus passed two stops. I stood up gasping for air and rushed to get off.

"This isn't your stop." The conductor said.

"Please stop the bus." I ran across the road looking for the bus stop to take me back home. I was aware of someone walking close to me.

"Jane." I looked around. It was Sybil, the woman I had been fostered to. "How are you keeping?"

"Alright."

"Where are you living?"

"In a flat up the road with my little boy. *Please* will you come and see us?"

"What, right now?"

"Yes, please." We started walking towards the flat.

"How old is your little boy?"

"Five. Are you coming back with me?"

"Yes, of course. I don't have much time though."

The flat was in sight. "This is it." I unlocked the front door. "It's upstairs." She followed me.

"God, this place is gloomy. Are there any lights?" On the first landing she pushed the bathroom door fully open. "How many people live here?"

"About eight."

"And that's the only toilet, is it?"

"Yes."

"Hmm that's obvious. It's filthy." We carried on up the stairs. "Do you pay rent for this?"

"Yes."

"I would have thought it's ready for demolition."

I moved the flat door to one side, it was still off its hinges. I watched as Sybil looked around.

"This is disgraceful. Where does your son sleep?"

"Here in bed with me. When we first got here, he slept in one of the drawers."

"How can anyone live like this? It's damp, dark, stomach churning."

I lowered my head.

"I'm not telling you off. Have you seen Mrs Roth recently?"

"No."

"I'll get in touch with her. You can't live like this. How is your son?"

"He has a very bad chest. He goes to see someone at the hospital."

"I'm not surprised."

The young man from the office next door returned from his holiday. I was walking to the Post Office, asking people for the time as I went.

"Ask me the time?" I recognised his voice and turned around, my head lowered.

"Hello."

"Did you go to the doctor? Did you do as I said?"

"Yes."

"Come on, we'll go for a Chinese. Then take it back to yours. I'll come in the back way, don't want anyone to see me."

I waited in the flat for him. "Jesus fucking Christ, It's not often you see rats milling around during the day."

We ate the meals. I could see him looking at me, I was wondering why.

"You're a strange one. Take off your coat." I started to take it off.

"Quicker than that, get everything off. I'm on my lunch break." Undressing quickly, I started sobbing, desperate to get into bed with him.

"Hey, hang on wait. Give me a minute to catch my breath. Looks like I'm gonna have to show you what to do."

As he was getting dressed, he leaned over the bed. "Hope you haven't given me anything. See you next week." He left the room. I ran to the window watching him.

The following week I bumped into him on the way back from the Post Office. "I'll be at yours in five minutes. I've got something for you."

I got into bed and waited for him.

"Why are you in bed? Come on put these on. I got them from the second-hand shop down the road. Why do you wear so many clothes?" I didn't answer. "Come on, put them on. I like my women to look like women." He handed me a bag. I pulled out a mini skirt and a pair of high heels. I put them on, I felt so sad without my clothes on, I sat on the edge of the bed and he jumped over the couch. We got into bed.

Each day was the same. About ten days later after taking my son to school I got back into bed. I had some Mars bars and crisps and frenziedly ate them. I heard footsteps on the stairs. "Someone must be moving in." I whispered closing my eyes.

"What are you doing in bed?" I looked up. It was the young man from the office. "Come on we'll go and get something to eat." I pushed the blankets back. "What the hell...You've still got the skirt and shoes on I brought you. Have you taken them off yet?"

"No. What's wrong?" I asked sobbing.

"It's a bit strange not to change your clothes."

"You said I looked nice. I like them, they make me feel comfortable." I whispered.

"I can't figure that one out." After about an hour he left the flat.

A few days later I heard footsteps on the bare floorboards. There was a knock on the door.

"Jane. Are you there?" I recognised the voice. It was Mrs Roth.

"Yes. I'm here, Mrs Roth." I got out of bed, watching as she looked around.

"Where's your son?"

"In school."

"Why is the door off the hinges?"

"I don't know."

"This place is a disgrace. How long have you lived here?"

"About three or four years."

"Do you see your brothers? Do they help you?"

"No. I don't know." I lowered my head.

"Well, this place is disgusting. I'll see what I can do." I watched as she took out a large pad from her briefcase. "Has your son had a *bris*?"

"No." I shrugged.

"Why not? It's important."

"I don't know."

"I think you should dress more appropriately. Wear a long skirt or trousers. You'll hear from me soon." I watched as she put her things back into her briefcase. I listened as the front door banged.

The following morning I took my son to school. I walked around the block to see if I could see the man from the office. It had been a week since I last saw him and I felt very sad. I got into bed with my food, bingeing. I knew he'd gone away. I held my breasts tightly before I managed to find the energy to go downstairs to the toilet and vomit till all the contents of my stomach were out. I sat on the toilet floor, my throat and head aching, my eyes and nose streaming with liquid, so weak I was only able to crawl back up the stairs.

A week passed, it was early morning and I heard footsteps on the stairs.

"Jane, it's Mrs Roth. I've been in touch with a local housing association. I've done a deal with them. Do you understand?"

"Yes."

"You must send your son to King David Junior school. You must bring him up in the Faith. You will have to take him to the synagogue. He will have to be circumcised. Do you understand what I'm saying?"

"Alright," I said, my gaze still fixed to the floor.

"I'll be in touch." She left the flat. I sat listening to her footsteps, descending the stairs.

CHAPTER 10

After taking my son to school, I went back to the flat and waited for Mrs Roth to leave the key for the new flat. Sitting on the bed, I waited till I heard the front door slam. I heard her footsteps on the stairs.

"Jane. Here are the keys. We've arranged for some donated furniture and carpets to be delivered and fitted tomorrow. You can move in any time after that."

"Thank you, Mrs Roth."

"You must make enquiries to have your son circumcised. He's going to feel awkward using the toilets in a Jewish school. All the other boys will have had a *bris*. Do you understand?"

"Yes." I said.

"I wanted the Jewish Social Services to buy you some new carpets. Mr Berman said no, he hasn't forgiven you for marrying out." I pictured Mr Berman's face from the Jewish Board of Guardians.

"They're also delivering a gas stove and twin tub washing machine."

"Thank you, Mrs Roth."

"I'm rushing to meet my daughter in town. Both my children married out. My husband won't have them in the house or have their names mentioned. Before I forget, the Jewish Social Services will give you a pound a week in assistance. That should help you."

She left the house. I sat holding the key. I waited for school to finish, then collected my son, picking up the few carrier bags with my belongings in. We made our way to our new home.

"We're going to live in a nice flat." I smiled at him.

"Where is it, Mummy?"

"It's near where I grew up. Come on, let's get the bus."

The bus arrived. He sat on my lap. "Please have you got the right time?" I asked a young woman sitting in front. I edged away as the conductor asked for my fare, "Please can you tell me when we get into town?"

We got off at Salford bus station and waited for the bus to take us up Cheetham Hill Road. I was to get off a few stops after the bus turned onto Middleton Road, then look for Catherine Road. My heart was pounding as the bus passed the old surgery. When I saw Smedley Lane and the house where my father's flat had been, my head filled with terrible darkness, smells and hunger which were so painful.

"What's the matter love?" A woman tapped me on the shoulder. I was sobbing. I said nothing except to ask her the time.

"Mummy, why are you crying?" I held his hand and cuddled him. As the bus made its way further up Cheetham Hill Road, the desperation got worse. Soon King David High School was in sight. I wanted to be in bed asleep, away from the world. We got off the bus and started walking.

"I'm hungry, Mummy."

"We'll go and buy some food from the shop over there." It was a kosher bakery. I held his hand tightly as I pushed the shop door open. I felt light headed. I heard people speaking *Yiddish*. I looked at the floor, knowing I didn't belong.

"Can I have some bagels and onion buns?"

"Pass me some *sybilibondies*," she asked another member of staff. "They're called *sybilibondies*."

"I know. I'm Jewish." I whispered. They looked at me. I paid and left the shop. Next door was a grocery shop. I bought some cheese and chocolate.

"I think this is the turning, down here." I had been told the flat overlooked the cricket ground off Middleton Road. We walked down Catherine Road. I could see a block of flats. We walked up a small flight of concrete stairs to the flat. I put the key in the lock, walking through the door there was a small bedroom. To the left a living-room and small kitchen. Further down the long hallway a bathroom and larger bedroom. It was a brand new flat. I went back and closed the front door. I sat in the corner of the living-room and curled up on the floor my son sat beside me.

"Are you going to *shloff*, Mummy?"

"Yes, be a good boy for mummy." A few hours later, I awoke. "Come on. We'll have something to eat." I looked through the bags. "You'll like these. They're bagels. I'll get you some pickled meat soon."

"What's that, Mum?"

After we had eaten I curled up on the floor, making the carrier bags into pillows for us.

"You be a good boy. Mummy loves you. Let's go to *shloff*."

The following day I saw the postman walk past the kitchen window. I ran into the hall, my heart pounding, to see if anyone had sent me a letter. There was nothing. We left the flat early. I knew everything was being delivered and the carpets fitted. We went to look for a doctor to register. I walked onto Cheetham

Hill Road, my head in a daze, trying hard not to look at Upper Park Road or the school.

"Have you got the right time please? Do you know where the nearest doctor's surgery is?" I asked someone passing.

"There's a doctor's surgery over the road. Doctor Bernstein."

"Thank you." After registering with the doctor, I found a hardware shop.

"Can I have a *ribizon* and *hackmesher*?"

"It's a long time since I've heard them called that." She looked at me. "You're *not* Jewish?"

We started walking again. "I'm going to make some chicken soup and meatballs for us."

When I got back to the flat, the carpets had been laid. The cooker and twin tub washing machine were in the kitchen, the beds had been delivered along with some bedding. All I needed was a table and chairs for the kitchen and couch for the living-room. Wardrobes and bedroom furniture could wait. The following morning was his first day at the new school. I held the wall as we approached the school playground, wanting to run away.

"Go in with the other children when the bell goes. I'll get you later."

"Mummy!"

I turned around. He was crying, running towards me.

"You've got to go to school. I'm going to make nice things for you. Be a good boy." I kissed him and left. The bell rang and I watched as he got into line, walking through the front doors. The urge to sleep was desperate. My eyes felt heavy. Looking around the area I noticed a shop, selling new and second-hand furniture and carpets. There was a small dining table and chairs in the window.

"How much is the table and chairs?"

"Forty five pounds."

"Can I buy it on credit?"

"I'm not sure about that. Where do you live? How long have you lived there?"

"A flat on Catherine Road. I moved in yesterday." He walked over to another man sitting at the back of the cluttered shop at a desk. I watched as he came back.

"No. I can knock five pounds off for cash."

"I haven't got it."

I started walking towards Greenhill Road to the butcher shop. The Kosher butchers were too expensive. I wanted some mincemeat and chicken so I could make meatballs and chicken soup for us. I was so tired. As soon as I arrived home I got into bed and slept. I wanted to go and make the chicken soup. "Don't worry Hikey, I'll do it later when you've had a *shloff*." Frenziedly I started eating the chocolate bars and cakes that I had bought for us. When I finished I went into the bathroom. "I need to *shloff* Hikey" I said. I hated myself so much I rammed my fingers down my throat. My body slouched to the floor, my heart pounding, crawling back to bed having just enough energy to get under the blankets. I could smell the urine. It comforted me as I fell asleep.

I woke up about mid-day with enough time to make the chicken soup. I felt so excited at the thought of sharing some with my son. A few days passed. I took my son to school.

"Mrs Levene." I looked up. One of the teachers was walking towards me.

"I don't want you to take this the wrong way but your son smells. Does he wet himself?"

"No."

"There seems to be a problem. People are noticing. Please make sure he comes to school in a decent state."

"Yes." I left the playground then went to buy some food. I didn't understand why the teacher had told me off. I got home and fell asleep. I was woken by a voice.

"Jane, where are you?" It was Mrs Roth. She walked into the bedroom.

"You left your front door open. Why are you in bed? Why have you got all your clothes on?"

I got out of bed and sat on it. "Have you been to see the doctor yet? Your son needs to be circumcised. I've arranged with the rabbi's wife for you to go to *shul* on Saturday with him. Clean yourself up. I've brought you some clothes."

"Thank you."

"Don't forget, Heaton Park Synagogue. Saturday morning."

"Yes, Mrs Roth."

I ran to the window and watched her get in the car and drive off. After a while I made some meatballs and put them in the oven. I stayed in bed till it was time to collect my son.

"Mummy's made some meatballs for tea. When I get some money, I'm going to buy a table and chairs so we can sit at the table. It will be like a party."

"Yes, Mummy that sounds nice."

"After tea you can have a bath. Won't that be nice for you?"

"Yes."

"I'm going to look for a part-time job so I can buy us nice things for the flat."

"And toys."

"Yes."

The following morning I noticed an advert in the local sweet shop for a part-time cleaner. I rang the number. "I'm ringing about the cleaning job."

"An hour three mornings a week, do you have experience?"

"Yes."

"What's your name?"

"Jane Levene."

"You're Jewish."

"Yes."

"I'm sorry. I'm Jewish. I can't have someone Jewish cleaning my home."

"Please, I'll do a good job."

"No." The phone slammed down.

I bought a local paper on the way home. There was an advert. I rang the number. A woman answered.

"I'm ringing about the job."

"Can you start tomorrow? I desperately need someone who can start immediately. An hour and a half, three times a week, start at nine."

"I have a little boy can I come after I take him to school?"

"Yes."

The house wasn't too far. It was a large house just like the children's home, my stomach churned as I approached the front door.

"Hello. I expect you to do a thorough job." A slender grey haired Jewish lady led me into the house.

"Yes, I promise."

"I'm rushing, I have an appointment. This is where the cleaning materials are kept." I followed her into the front lounge. "This is my husband." He was a grey haired man sitting in a wheel chair. "I have a friend who's looking for a cleaner. Two hours once a week. Can you do it?"

"Yes, please. I want to buy a table and chairs."

"I'll let her know. I'm off." I heard the front door slam. I collected all the cleaning materials and started in the bedrooms and worked down. I entered the lounge.

"Come here!" the husband shouted.

"I've got to finish my work." The phone rang. I could hear him talking.

"Where are you?"

"I'm here."

"Here's the address of our friend. It's not far from here. Come tomorrow morning. Then you can go there when you have finished."

"OK." I quickly took the piece of paper off him, trying hard not to inhale the smell of his body.

I rushed home wanting to see if the postman had been back, perhaps there was a letter from Jeffery. There was nothing. I slept till it was time to collect my son from school. When he saw me he ran to me.

"Mummy's got a job. I'm going to buy some nice things for the flat. I'll buy you a police car and some sweets on Friday."

The following morning I heard a letter being pushed through the letterbox. Hurriedly I rushed to get it. My heart sank when I realised it was a bill. I made my way to work, on the way I decided to buy some chocolate. On the counter there was a pile of cards shaped like cocoa beans and coffee beans. I looked at them. "Fill in the information on the back and they'll send you a free sample of something," the shopkeeper said. I picked up two forms and went to the Post Office and posted them. I hoped they would write to me soon.

I went to work. The woman was about to leave the house.

"I have to go shopping. Are you going to my friend's house when you finish here?"

"Yes."

"She's a very nice woman. See you." The door slammed. I started my work.

"Come here!" I walked into the lounge. My heart pounding, I felt faint.

"You're a nice looking *shiksa*."

"I'm not a *shiksa*." I frowned. Dark feelings came over me.

"How do you know what *shiksa*. means? You're not Jewish."

"Yes, I am."

"My wife wouldn't have someone Jewish cleaning," I looked away.

"Come here. I want to show you something. Come here, I said" He looked very angry. I wanted to force some food down my throat. "Jane Levene." I whispered as I reluctantly started walking towards him. I knew he couldn't get out of his wheel chair. As I got closer he pulled something from under his cushion.

"Here look at this book." He held up a picture of a naked woman. "Come and look at it with me."

"No." My heart racing, I ran out of the house.

The next job was only a ten minute walk. My head was still reeling as I knocked on the door.

"Hello, you must be Jane."

"Yes."

"Come in." I followed a very large Jewish woman into the kitchen.

"It's *Erev Yom Tov* tonight. That means it's a major holiday for Jewish people tomorrow."

"I know." I mumbled.

"How would you know? Have you worked for Jewish people before?" I said nothing. "I was cooking till the early hours of the morning. I need to do some more shopping. You know what to do. I'll be back later."

I got all the cleaning things out of the cupboard. I thought about the man with the magazine. I closed my eyes to stop thinking about him, but his face and smell were going round and round in my head.

"I hate you Jane Levene, you're not Jewish. Who do you think you are?" My head filled with dark self-loathing, my throat and stomach needed food. I opened the fridge door. There was a large bowl. I recognised what was in it, homemade chopped liver. There was no bread in the house because it was *Pesach*. Finding some Matzo, I spread a small amount on the Matzo and ate it. It felt so good in my tummy. I needed more. Soon the bowl was half empty. After another ten minutes it was almost empty. I didn't know what to do. I left the house quickly before she returned.

On my way home I joined the bus queue "Have you got the right time, please?" I asked an old Jewish lady in front of me.

"11 o'clock," she replied.

I started walking towards the flat. I noticed some adverts in the post office window. There was one for a morning cleaner. I applied and was told to start the following day. It was mid-winter. It had been snowing overnight, it was freezing. I found the house and knocked on the door. A man appeared. I could smell his body.

"Come in. My wife's in hospital. I'm rushing around at the moment. I'll show you where the cleaning cupboard is."

I followed him. The house was freezing cold. He told me what to do and left the house. I went upstairs. My breath was steaming as I breathed in and out. My hands were so cold it was difficult to hold the cloths. I went into the kitchen to put my hands under the hot water tap. The water ran cold. I sat in the living-room huddled under my coat shivering. The atmosphere felt dark and my head ached.

The front door opened. Immediately I jumped off the couch and hurried into the kitchen.

"Have you finished?"

"Yes. There was no hot water to mop the floor. It's very cold in the house."

"Did you mop the floors?"

"Yes."

"What are you moaning about then?"

"Nothing."

"Here's a pound. See you next week."

As I walked back to the flat along Middleton Road I noticed a postcard in a shop window. I looked closer it was an advert for a cleaner 'plus.' I wrote down the number.

"Hello?" a woman said in broken English.

"Hello, I'm ringing about the cleaning job."

"Have you experience?"

"Yes."

"I need someone to start immediately. Can you do that?"

"Yes."

"Are you reliable?"

"Yes, I need the money. I want to work."

"Can you start in the morning? Nine thirty."

"Yes please."

The following morning I walked to the house. Knocking on the front door I noticed the *Mezzuzah*. A woman opened the door. She was wearing a *sheitle*.

"Come in. We are Jewish people. I will train you in our ways." She beckoned me to follow her into the kitchen. "We have two kitchens, one for meat and one for milk. Each kitchen has its own cloths for cleaning. It is our custom not to mix them. That would be very bad. Do you understand?"

"Yes."

There was a portrait of a rabbi on the wall.

"That is my husband."

My legs started to shake. I could see her mouth moving but I wasn't listening.

"I need you to work two mornings a week. Can you do that?"

"Yes."

"Friday afternoon it is our Sabbath. I would like you to come and turn my gas stove on."

"A *Shabbas Goy*."

"Excuse me?"

"A *Shabbas Goy*."

"How do you know what a *Shabbas Goy* is?"

"I'm Jewish." I lowered my head slightly.

"Never, I don't believe you. Everyone wants to be Jewish these days. It's a fashion."

She left the house. I went into the milk kitchen. I picked up the cloth and rushed to the meat kitchen. Hurriedly, I cleaned everything in sight with the milk cloth. "I am Jewish, I'm not Jewish. I'm British not English" I was crying. On the way home I passed a newsagents I looked at the adverts in the window. Once again I noticed one for a morning cleaner, writing down the number I rushed to the phone box.

"Hello, may I help you?"

It was a woman's voice, I could tell she was Jewish.

"I've seen your advert for a cleaner."

"Oh yes, that's correct." She replied. "Do you have references?"

"No. But I work hard."

"I prefer to have references. Where do you live?"

"At the top of Cheetham Hill Road. I promise I'll do a good job, please give me a chance," I said, my heart pounding.

"OK, start tomorrow. If I'm happy with your work, you can have the job."

On the way home I collected my son from school. We walked home. He was telling me about his homework. The teacher had asked the children if their parents read them bedtime stories. He asked me if I could read him a story to make him sleep better. I didn't answer.

The following morning I arrived at the house. It was very large, it reminded me of the children's homes. My heart sank, I felt light headed as I knocked on the door. A Jewish woman opened the front door. I could smell the children's home. I followed her into the kitchen.

"I am recovering from having a breast removed so I need a good reliable cleaner." She looked at me sternly. I nodded.

"Yes." I replied.

"My name is Mrs Radnor. What's your name again?"

"Jane."

"Right Jane, follow me." She took me to a large room next to the kitchen, it had lots of kitchen units and cupboards.

"Everything you need is in here. I want you to start from the top floor down. The house is on different levels, there is a bathroom on the second level. Come, I'll show you." The house was so big it made me feel very cold and hungry.

It was a few hours before I finished all the work. The last room was the kitchen. When I walked in she was spooning some large pieces of *gefilte* fish and carrots out of a pan.

"These are fish balls, they say mine are the sweetest, most delicate they have ever tasted."

I carried on working. When I had finished I waited for her. She appeared.

"I can do without this," she was muttering. She looked at me. "My husband's gone to St Anne's today to buy a house for £75,000. He's paying cash, not that we need another house. My son's going out with a *shiksa*. His father will cut him off if he marries her. He won't get anything. Not one penny! I can do without all this aggravation, I haven't been well." She took some liver out of the fridge and started frying it.

"Can I ask you a question?"

"Yes, be quick, I'm busy. I need you here five mornings."

"That's OK. Do you have a shoe factory?" I asked her.

"Yes, we do. How do you know that?"

"When I was little, I remember my mum getting a voucher for my shoes. From the Jewish Benevolent Society. We took the voucher to Radnor's shoe factory."

"You're not Jewish?" She acted surprised. "I've never heard of a Jewish woman cleaning. Not in my house. I'll show you out."

I didn't look for any more cleaning jobs.

CHAPTER 11

Life carried on, taking my son to school, buying food, going home to sleep, collecting him from school, asking people the time as I walked there and back. One day on the way back to the flat I saw someone approaching that I recognised from the club where I had been working.

"They're opening a new club, it's in town. They want staff. Give them a ring. They pay cash in hand." I rang the club and was told to start on Friday.

Friday evening I waited till it was time to leave for work. I put my long dark coat on over my mini skirt and put on my high heels. I knew the coat would hide me. It was very hot and busy in the club. A few hours passed and my feet were hurting badly. They were itchy, hot and painful. I wished I could take my shoes off but they were part of me. The man I had met when I was in the flat on Bolton Road had told me that I looked nice and sexy with them on.

Saturday morning arrived. I dressed my son in some of the clothes Mrs Roth had brought. "We've got to go to *shul.*" I said frowning. I couldn't contain the sobs.

"What's that, Mummy? What's wrong Mummy?"

I couldn't answer. The terrible feelings at the thought of going to *shul* made my head ache but I knew I must, that was why I had been given the flat. "Jane Levene. I hate you" I whispered. I wore a pair of red wide leg trousers and a green leather jacket.

"Come on. We'll have to go."

I stood outside the synagogue with my son holding his hand, desperate, not knowing what to do. I hated myself. "You're nothing Levene the smelly thing, you stink, *ipish*." I mumbled.

"What, Mummy?"

"Nothing." I whispered, my heart banging. I waited, trying to summon up the courage to go in. I watched as a woman approached me. She was wearing a *sheitle* and was obviously *frum.*

"Are you Jane Levene?"

"Yes."

"Mrs Roth told me to expect you. You can't come into the synagogue wearing trousers. You must have something on your head. Go home get changed. Come back, hurry!"

Walking home I looked to see how much money I had. There was enough for some crisps and chocolate.

"Come on. Let's go to bed. Mummy loves you."

Sunday mid-morning, someone was knocking at the door.

"Jane. Open the door. It's Mrs Roth."

My heart sank. I wanted to stuff my stomach full of food.

"I had a word with the rabbi's wife. Why didn't you go back to *shul*? Is your son circumcised?" She sounded very angry.

"Sorry."

"Sorry isn't really good enough. There are other people who need help. Not just you. Have you registered with a doctor?"

"Yes."

"Did you mention the circumcision to the doctor?"

"No."

"Go and get it arranged. Consider your son. How do you think he will feel when he uses the toilet and all the other boys have had a *bris*?"

I watched out of the window as she got into her car. I hoped that she would look back and smile but she didn't. I waited till the car was out of sight.

"Mummy needs to go to the toilet. You stay here. I won't be long." I rushed to the kitchen grabbing any food I could find. As soon as I locked the bathroom door my heart started racing. I put the taps on, got on the floor, pulled down my trousers. I didn't know who the body belonged to. I felt wet dribbling down my legs. I forced all the food I had down my throat. I felt too weak to get up and retched on the floor. I knew my face was swollen and wet. As I got up I felt completely drained of energy.

I made an appointment to see Dr Bernstein. I waited till my name was called. All the old feelings came flooding over me.

"How are you today?"

"I think I've got asthma."

"Why do you think that?"

"Because a lot of the time I gasp for air, I can't breathe."

"Lift your jumper." He examined my chest using a stethoscope. "There doesn't appear to be a spasm. I'll give you a prescription for 'Becotide.' You have a severe skin rash here on your neck. I can give you some treatment."

I started crying. "My mum's dead."

"Is there something else?"

"My throat's sore. I don't feel well."

He examined my throat. "Your throat is red raw. That's a nasty infection."

"I feel very ill."

"You need some antibiotics. I see you're on the pill. Are you sexually active?"

"What?"

"Do you have sex?"

"No." I replied lowering my head.

"Have you had a smear test?"

"No."

"Make an appointment with the receptionist for the smear test."

"Thank you, Doctor. Can I ask you something else?"

"What is it?"

"My son needs a circumcision."

"Why?"

"Mrs Roth said because he's going to a Jewish school."

"How old is he?"

"Six."

"To be honest, it's risky and painful at that age. It's your choice."

"I won't bother."

I returned for the smear test. Doctor Bernstein told me to make another appointment to see him in three weeks' time. He carried out another smear test.

I got to the surgery. I felt comforted counting the pictures on the wall and the chairs. I was waiting for my appointment. The receptionist called my name.

"Doctor Bernstein will see you now."

I entered his surgery.

"Go and get ready." He pointed to the small examination room.

"We'll just have a peep. You must keep coming back. We have to keep an eye on you. We don't want you to get cancer do we?"

"No, Doctor Bernstein."

Months passed. There was a knock on the door, it was Mrs Roth.

"You've been sleeping haven't you?"

"Yes, on the couch."

"You look a mess. You smell of urine. Do something with yourself. Have you seen your brothers?"

"No."

"Have you got any friends?"

"No. Andrea came to visit me, she stayed here overnight with her son. I made them chicken soup. They enjoyed it."

"Andrea who?"

"I lived with them after Auntie Doris."

"Yes, I remember. How often do you see her?"

"I've only seen her once. She doesn't want her sister to know or she'll get very angry. I like her, she reminds me of Minnie Shelefski."

"Who? Never mind. Anyway I want you to meet someone. Listen to what I'm saying. He's a Jewish man. He's very nice, his name is Tony. He has his own house, you'll be well looked after. His wife died in childbirth. He has a son about the same age as yours. You can look after them both. I'll pick you up tomorrow evening at seven o'clock. He's going to cook you a meal. Do you have a baby sitter?"

"Yes, I'll give the woman next door the key."

The following day I took my son to school. I bought some food and went home. Staying in bed all day, I didn't want to think about what was happening. I heard knocking on the front door.

"Jane, it's Mrs Roth." I opened the door. "You look presentable. Come on."

I sat in the car, looking out of the window. I knew I didn't belong to Mrs Roth. I wanted to be at home comfortable and warm on the couch.

"This is the house. Knock on the door. Go on."

I walked down the path, my heart pounding. I felt so cold and hungry. I knocked on the door. I didn't like the smell that was wafting as I lifted the letter box. Turning around, Mrs Roth's car had gone.

"You must be Jane. I'm Tony. Come in. I hope you like chicken soup. Do you like Matzo balls?"

I tried to smile but found it difficult to lift my head. I followed him into the house. I listened as the door slammed.

"Sit down while I finish the meal." I sat on his couch afraid to inhale, gasping for breath.

"Go and freshen up. The bathroom's upstairs."

I walked up the stairs, his bedroom door was open. I saw his dirty socks on the floor. I could smell them, I could smell his body. I ran down the stairs, quickly opening the front door. "Mummy, mummy" I sobbed running home. Soon the flat was in sight. I collected my key from the next door neighbour.

My son was fast asleep in my bed. I got in with him cuddling him. His eyes opened.

"*Gehen shloffen*. Mummy needs to sleep. Love you."

"Love you too Mummy."

The following morning after taking him to school I went home. I got on the couch and curled up. My body odours comforted me. My eyes were closing. I was woken with a jolt.

"Jane, you left your front door open again. Why on earth are you lying on the couch in that state? I can smell you from here." I sat up. "Why did you run out of Tony's house?"

"I don't know."

"I went to a lot of trouble to arrange that meeting. How do you think Tony felt? That is a disgusting way to treat such a nice man. Do you know what he's been through? Do you understand anything? Why are you so self-centred?" I lowered my head. "Yes, you should look sheepish! You should be ashamed of yourself. I'm losing patience."

"I'm sorry, Mrs Roth. Honestly."

"I've arranged a part-time job for you at the Jewish Social Services. It'll give you some extra money. Start on Monday two o'clock. Friday we close early for *Shabbas*."

"Thank you, Mrs Roth."

One morning I took my son to school. I waited in the playground as usual with him until the bell rang.

"Mrs Levene. I need a word." I looked at her with all the dread and stomach churning anxiety I had ever known. I knew she didn't like me and that she was only pretending to be nice and clean.

"I would like you to help your son with his homework. He's bright, he needs your help."

I walked onto Cheetham Hill Road to the television rental shop and ordered a television.

I found Holland Road. The Jewish Social Services was in a small office block. I entered the main door. My head lowered. I could hear voices. I walked into the main office. I could smell the children's home. Two young women sat at their typewriters talking. An older woman was looking at some letters.

"Hello. Who are you?"

"Jane Levene." I said with all the usual self-loathing.

"I'm Mrs Savage."

"Hello."

"Mrs Roth told me you married out."

"Yes."

"All you're fit for is cleaning toilets. The cleaning cupboard is off the corridor, clean the toilets first then the offices." I didn't have to lift my head to know that the two young Jewish women were giggling. I could hear them.

"Hello, Mr Berman." I heard Mrs Savage say.

I looked up. I recognised him. When the Jewish Board of Guardians opened on a Sunday morning he would open a hatch in the wall. *You may all go upstairs now,* he would say as he unlocked the room with all the second-hand clothes and items. He left the room. The women started talking.

"He's such a gentleman, Mr Berman. He takes his hat off when he makes love to his wife." They all laughed.

The following day when I arrived for work I noticed Mr Berman shouting as he dashed from his office. He was holding a tin of paint.

"Come here." I looked around not knowing if he was talking to me. "You, yes you. Come here." I walked towards his office, my heart pounding. "Take this tin of paint. Someone's written anti-Semitic rubbish on the pavement near the Yeshivah. I want you to paint over it." He looked very angry.

I hurried along the road till I could see the writing on the pavement. *Good news for Jews plastic surgery free on the NHS.* I knelt down and started painting over the writing.

"What do you think you are doing?" I looked up a policeman was standing over me. I looked at him.

"Mr Berman told me to do it."

"What's your address?"

I started crying. "Mr Berman told me to do it honestly. He's down the road at the Jewish Social Services."

"I think we'd better go and see Mr Berman."

I followed him to the office, tears streaming down my face. Mr Berman was in the reception area. I watched as he showed the policeman to his office. I was trembling, wondering who would collect my son from school if I was in prison. Soon they came out of the office.

"Go home." Mr Berman shouted. I ran all the way back to the flat and slept till it was time to collect my son from school.

A few weeks into the job, I went to work earlier than usual. There was a staff meeting and everyone was in the large office. I started cleaning the offices and noticed a row of files underneath the worktop. I knelt down and started looking at the files. I found a card with my name on. My heart started pounding. I searched through them picking out the ones with my name on.

"I hate you. I hate you." I repeated as I ripped them up and put them in my coat pocket. I noticed one with Auntie Doris's name on, it read: *She is finding it hard to cope and is requesting help.* My heart sank. She needed me. I must go and see her. Sobbing uncontrollably, I noticed a large blue ledger book it was open. It had lists of names. I was there: *Jane Levene one pound per week assistance.* Under my name was Wilfred Levene my father, he was receiving two pounds a week. I started shaking, my mind flashing back to his naked body. Moving away from the book, my body still shaking. I held the work top crying so hard, my eyes and nose streaming.

"What's going on?" I heard Mrs Savage's voice. "Go home."
She shouted.

I turned around she was standing there with the two
young women. My body was convulsing and trembling.

"Stop it," she insisted.

I ran out of the building and headed for the school. My
son was waiting for me.

"Are we having chicken soup tonight, Mum?"

"Yes. Mummy loves you." We walked to the shop. His hand
tugged at mine.

"I can't have that car in the window, can I Mum?"

"Not till I've got some money."

"I know that. Have you made some meatballs?"

"Yes."

Saturday morning we stayed in bed for a while.

"We'll go for a walk and buy some food. I'll buy you a
teacake in the café."

We set off down Cheetham Hill Road. I watched people
walking on both sides of the road. I didn't know any of them. I
watched them talking to each other. I felt very sorry for the ones
on their own because they didn't have anyone. I knew how they
felt. I sat on a bench holding my son's hand. There was no house
I could go to. No-one I could visit. I was trying to be everyone
to my son: mother, father, uncles and grandparents.

"Have you got the right time please?" I asked people
passing by. I remembered the file I had seen with Auntie Doris's
message on.

"We'll go and see Auntie Doris. She's not very happy. I love
Auntie Doris." I was faint as I approached her front door. My
heart was banging in my throat as she opened it.

"What do *you* want?"

"I've got a nice flat at the top of Cheetham Hill Road. Will you come and visit us? I'll make some chicken soup and braised steak." She looked at my son but said nothing.

"When?"

"Thursday next week."

"Fine, give me your address. I've got to go. I'm busy."

"See you soon, Auntie Doris."

When we got home I put the television on. An Open University programme was about to start, perhaps I could learn something so I could help my son with his homework, I thought to myself. I listened to what was being said but my mind started racing, I had visions of school, not understanding what was said or being able to answer questions when it was test or exam time. I watched the man on the television I could hear the words but couldn't take them in. My stomach churned and my head ached so much I went to sleep.

Days passed. I got my son ready for school.

"Auntie Doris is coming tonight for her tea. We can all sit at the table. I'll get some shopping and make some nice things."

He started crying. "Is she my grandma?"

"No."

"Have I got a grandma?"

"No. We've only got Auntie Doris. She's coming tonight. She'll love you, I'm sure."

I collected him from school. "Mummy, is Auntie Doris still coming for tea?"

"Yes." I replied. As soon as we got home I started making the meal. My son came into the kitchen. He started crying again.

"Is Jeffery and David coming?"

"No." I replied. "You stay in the living-room. Read your books. I'm going to make tea."

The food was ready. I looked out of the window to see if I could see her.

"Help mummy put knives and forks on the table."

"Mummy, what does this mean?" He held the book up. I couldn't look at it my stomach churned at the sight of the book. I felt dark, cold and hungry.

"I don't know." I stayed near to the window. She should have been here by now. There was no sign. I gave my son his meal. An hour passed then two hours. Still I kept looking out of the window.

"Why are you crying, Mummy?"

"I'm not. I've got something in my eye. Come on we'll go out for a walk. We'll get some chocolate." We walked along Middleton Road. The shops were all closed. "Have you got the right time?" I asked several people as we walked back to the flat.

I bought the local paper and noticed a job being advertised for box makers from 10 a.m till 1 p.m. I rang and was told I could start the day after. I found the 'Baracuda' factory in Ancoats. The building was huge. I got in the lift and pressed the button for the top floor, it didn't have doors just a huge iron gate, each floor it passed I could see rows and rows of sewing machines. The smell of machines made my tummy feel empty. I couldn't help but sob. I was met by the manager and I followed him to his office. He was a middle aged man.

"I need a job. I need some money to buy things for my flat. I've got a little boy." I said.

"Are you on benefits?"

"Yes."

"Hmm, I think we can come to an arrangement. I'll pay you in your hand."

"Thank you," I replied.

He took me to a huge table near a huge window that was broken. It was very cold and draughty in the room. He brought over a bundle of brown flat cardboard shapes and showed me how to make them into boxes. After a few hours my hands were cut in several places as they came into contact with the raw edges. A few days later the manager called me into his office.

"I want you to help bring some stock from the basement."

He smiled at me. I knew he needed me. I followed him. He unlocked a small door in the basement.

"Lie down on there." He pointed to an old work bench.

"Daddy," the words repeated in my head. I did what he asked and closed my eyes as he sat over me. I looked away. Why was he doing this to me, what had I done wrong? the words repeating in my head. He told me to go back to work. I finished my shift and left the building. On the way home I collected my son from school. I held his hand and we started to walk back to the flat.

"What had I done wrong?" I mumbled repeatedly.

"Are you OK, Mum?"

"Yes, mummy's fine." Once home I put the television on and sat my son on the sofa.

"Mummy needs to wee. You stay there. Be a good boy."

I went into the kitchen and filled my pockets with food. I needed to get into the bathroom to stuff it all down my throat to ease the pain. I looked in the mirror. I still had food in my mouth. My heart was pounding and I felt weak. "I hate you." I whispered repeatedly. I opened my coat and pulled my trousers down to my knees. Hitting myself between my legs with my shoe I knew I had to get all the food out of my stomach. I rubbed my finger on some soap and stuck it down my throat. Soon my body heaved as all the food came back, all the moisture coming from my eyes and nose was dribbling down my neck. I laid on the floor for a while. I opened the bathroom door.

"Mummy's coming, we'll have a *shloff.*" I shouted. I got on the couch and pulled him close. "Mummy loves you more than anything in the world. I'll never leave you. I promise." Soon we both fell asleep.

A few weeks' later the manager told me that the job was only temporary and that I had to finish.

CHAPTER 12

There was a knock on the front door. I could see it was Mrs Roth. I opened the door, my heart racing. I didn't know if I had done something wrong.

"Hello, Mrs Roth." She rushed past me to the living-room. I felt my wrist to make sure I was still alive.

"Mrs Savage said there have been complaints about your behaviour at the office recently. I'm going to take you to meet someone on Monday morning. He's a psychiatrist. I've also arranged for you to meet a young woman, about your age with a small child. She's divorced. That's been arranged for the week after next."

"OK. Thank you Mrs Roth." She rushed to the front door and I watched as she drove off.

Mrs Roth arrived on Monday morning. My mind was blank as we made the journey to the hospital, petrified I was going to have my son taken from me.

"This is the hospital." I followed her as she hurriedly walked down the grey corridors.

"I think this is the room. Go on. Knock on the door. I'll wait here for you."

I went into a small office, a Jewish man was sitting behind a desk. I cowered and veered towards the wall, not wanting to get a hint of his body smells. My head lowered. I wanted to run away.

"Sit down." He looked at me. There was a long silence as

he looked through his notes. "Why did you marry out?" He asked insistently.

"I don't know."

"Aren't there enough Jewish men in the world for you?"

My head was lowered. I sat, not knowing what to say. It was too difficult to speak. I sensed he was moving around. I heard the door open. He spoke to Mrs Roth. His voice lowered.

"She's unresponsive, of low intelligence."

We drove back to the flat. "Be ready next Sunday ten o'clock. I'll take you to meet Rachel and her little boy. She's a very nice young woman. Very pleasant, I'm sure you'll enjoy her company."

"Yes, Mrs Roth."

My head felt very dark and heavy. I knew the woman was only pretending to be nice. Mrs Roth believed her. The door slammed. I rushed to the window to watch the car. Quickly I went into the kitchen, looking through the cupboards pulling everything out. Sitting on the floor, I stuffed everything in my mouth. My eyes and nose started to stream even though I hadn't stuck my fingers down my throat. I felt the wet between my legs. "Mummy, mummy." I mumbled as I made my way to the bathroom. I stuck my fingers down my throat not stopping till there was only clear liquid coming from my stomach. I looked in the mirror I could see my mother. "I love you Hikey. Don't worry." I curled up in the corner of the bathroom. I tried to get up but felt so weak. I crawled to the living-room, got on the couch and covered myself with my coat. "Love you Mummy." I closed my eyes and fell asleep.

Sunday arrived. I looked out of the window. Mrs Roth was in her car. After a while she looked up, beckoning me to the car. She looked very angry. I rushed to the car.

"I've not got all day. What kept you?"

"Sorry."

"Are you taking care of yourself?"

"Yes."

"Do you have a bath regularly?"

"Yes."

"Remember this young woman is in the same situation as you. She's divorced. You need to make friends."

"Yes, Mrs Roth."

Soon we were at Rachel's house. I felt hungry and cold, needing to eat. Rachel opened the door and I followed Mrs Roth into the house.

"Jane, this is Rachel."

Mrs Roth knew Rachel was a nice name, I could tell by her smile. I lowered my head. She knew I was Jane Levene. She hated me as much as I did.

"I'm going. I'll call back at lunchtime."

My heart sank as Mrs Roth left the house. I didn't like it here. It didn't smell right. I wanted to go home to bed.

"Would you like a cup of tea and some cake?"

"Yes please." My head still lowered. She handed me the tea and cake. I watched as she ate hers nicely. I was so hungry it was difficult not to eat it quickly.

"That was good, thank you."

I didn't lift my head. She knew I was horrible. I waited for Mrs Roth to come back. I said nothing.

My life continued as normal, taking my son to school. Buying food, going home to sleep on the couch, wearing three or four jumpers and my coat, it was difficult to stay warm without them even in summer.

Mrs Roth visited. "I'd like you to meet another psychiatrist. This one is a woman. I've made arrangements for you to see her next week. I'll take you there."

The following week we made the journey to Prestwich Hospital. We got out of the car and walked along the path. A large woman greeted us. I looked at her clothes. She was wearing a long flowing colourful skirt, shirt with a matching scarf wrapped around her head. She was big with black hair, just like my mum. I wished she could have had some nice clothes. It was obvious they liked each other. I turned away. I knew they didn't want me there.

"Jane, I want you to go and have a word with Claire."

"Come on dear, my office is down this corridor. Sit down. Would you like a coffee?"

"No thank you." I said, looking at the floor.

"Your mother's dead."

"Yes."

"Mrs Roth tells me you have two brothers." My face screwed up, I instantly held my breasts. She remained silent for a while.

"You're holding your breasts? You turn to yourself for comfort. Can you explain your behaviour?"

"Don't know."

"Do you see your brothers? Mrs Roth told me one is older and the other younger?"

"Yes."

"Do you see your older brother? Where does he live?"

"I don't see him, I don't know where he lives."

"Does he visit you?"

"No." I lowered my head. My gaze remained on the floor. My heart pounding and my head full of dark desperation.

After a while she stood up beckoning me over to the door. Mrs Roth was waiting for me.

"She needs a mother. She's never been nurtured. She seems to get comfort from herself. She holds her own breasts."

I stood near the wall my head still lowered. Mrs Roth dropped me on Cheetham Hill Road and I waited till school finished and collected my son. After we had eaten we went to bed.

"Let mummy *shloff*. Be a good boy. Love you."

My visits to Doctor Bernstein became a regular occurrence. Every four or five weeks I would make an appointment to see him. Each time he carried out a smear test telling me to book another for the following month. On the way back from one of the visits I saw Morris approaching.

"How are you?"

"Fine. I've got a job."

"Where, what are you doing?"

"Cleaning. I think I'll have to finish. I can't pick my son up from school early on Friday's. There's no one to collect him for me. How's David?"

"*Nisht gut.* Jeffery isn't a good influence on him. Anita thinks you would be better for him. I'm retired now, I can pick him up from school, you can collect him from our house. Have a word with David, it might do him a bit of good."

"OK. Thank you."

As promised, Morris collected my son from school. I bought a box of cream cakes for them by way of thanks. I got off the bus, walking towards their house. Feeling faint, I gasped for air so it could fill my lungs. If I were to die my son would be left without a mother. I had searing feelings of icy coldness in my head as I approached the front door. David let me in. My son was sitting on the floor. I put the box of cakes down on the small coffee table. David sat in front of the television, Morris was reading his paper. I could see the cigarette smoke rising behind it.

"He's had something to eat." Anita said. "He needs some decent food in him. Morris is doing this because he's a *mensch*. I hope you appreciate it. You could have had a good husband if you'd have married Ivan. Most women in your position would jump at the chance. David's cousins are very clever, they're going to be successful in life. Why don't you go to night school? Do something with your life. Toilet cleaning isn't a nice *Yiddishy* trade." The words came out of her mouth like machine gun bullets, each one a thunderous kick to my head which was difficult to recover from.

The phone rang. Anita rushed in from the kitchen. "Morris, Morris, there's a man on the phone. He wants to know if I've got hair between my legs." Morris kept on reading the paper the cigarette smoke still climbing over it. "Morris!" He lowered the paper and shrugged his shoulders. He didn't reply.

I went to work as usual. Mrs Roth was talking to a man in the corridor. I cowered away from them and touched the wall for comfort.

"Jane, I want you to meet David Lewis. He's taking over as Director of the Jewish Social Services now that Mr Berman has retired. Jane remembers when Mr Berman ran the Jewish Board of Guardians." Mrs Roth said. I looked away.

"Hello, Jane," he said. "This is my wife." She was slim, blonde and attractive.

"Hello." I replied half smiling.

He took her arm and they headed towards the front door.

"She's not Jewish. She's been *magiyed*. He married out. It's a sign of the times. What can you do!" Mrs Roth said. I looked at the floor.

Months passed. Mrs Roth came to see me. "I've brought your son some clothes. We received them yesterday." She placed a small brown box on the floor. "I see you have a new carpet."

"Yes, I bought it. I got a job to get some money. I've got a table and chairs in the kitchen and a coffee table."

"The flat looks very nice. You've done well. How's your son?"

"He's fine."

"Has he been circumcised?"

"No. The doctor said..."

"Stop there. I think you're really selfish. How do you think he feels when he's in the toilets with the other boys? I give up with you." I could see she wasn't pleased.

"Sorry, Mrs Roth."

"It's your son you should be apologising to."

I was still working at the Jewish Social Services. As usual Morris collected my son on Friday afternoon. It was his birthday and I bought him a large birthday cake and a battery operated police car. I wanted him to have a birthday party. I told the neighbour who had babysat for me to bring her daughter so they could have some birthday cake. She was heavily pregnant and wasn't able to come. He started crying.

"Mummy, does Uncle Jeffery and David know it's my birthday?"

"No."

"Is David coming for some cake?"

"I don't think so."

"Are they going to buy me a present?" He sobbed.

"No."

"Don't they like me?"

"You've got mummy. I love you very much." I tried to reassure him.

A few weeks' passed and David called to see me.

"Morris can't collect him from school on Friday. He can't do it anymore."

"OK."

"He's bought a great television. It's huge. It was cheap, he got it discounted."

About a month later David rang.

"Morris is really pissed off. The police have been round. That bloody television had been stolen from Manchester City Football Club. It was in the footballers lounge. They've confiscated it. He won't get his money back."

I had been living in the flat for about eighteen months. Mrs Roth called to see me. "There's a disco at the Jewish Lads Brigade next week. I'd like you to go and see if you can meet a nice Jewish boy." She looked at me. "You need to try to meet someone Jewish. I brought you some clothes, they were donated recently, have a look at them. They should fit you."

I looked in the box. Why had she brought them for me? I wanted to sleep.

"Make sure you look smart."

She left the details of the disco with me. "I'll be in touch."

I looked out of the window as she drove off.

"What's the matter, Mummy?"

"Nothing, let's go to *shloff*."

I put one of the jumpers on that Mrs Roth had brought and made my way to the disco. I approached the JLB with all the same fear that I had done in the past. I walked through the main doors, paid my entrance fee. I bought myself a bottle of cola and sat in the corner for a while. I watched the young people dancing.

"I remember you from school?"

Looking up I recognised the face without remembering the name. He sat next to me. I moved away.

"Can I join you? What are you doing with yourself these days?"

"I'm divorced. I have a little boy. We live not far from here."

"Do you work?"

"I had a job collecting glasses."

"If you need any extra money, I have a friend who can get you on the game."

I didn't reply.

The following day I went to work. Mrs Roth was in the office.

"Did you go to the JLB dance?"

"Yes."

"Did you meet anyone?"

"No."

"What's the matter with you? You need to try a lot harder."

"Yes, Mrs Roth."

"Here, I've kept these newspaper clippings for you. One is a Jewish house party taking place this weekend. The other is an advert looking for people to host a Jewish house party. I want you to do your best." She looked stern.

"Yes, Mrs Roth."

I made arrangements for my next door neighbour to babysit. I found the address. The house was a very large house in Whitefield. I didn't like the house. The dark, damp, cold, feelings made me want to eat. Knocking on the door I tried to fill my lungs with air. I knew Mrs Roth would be very unhappy if I didn't meet a nice Jewish boy. I knocked on the door. A young Jewish woman opened the door.

"Can I help you?"

"I've come for the house party."

"This is for Jewish people. I think you'll feel a bit out of place."

"I'm Jewish. Mrs Roth told me to come."

"Mrs Who?"

"Roth."

"You don't look Jewish. Are you *unzury*. One of us?"

"Yes."

She showed me to a table that was full of bottles of wine. She poured me a glass and handed it to me. The rooms were so large I could smell the Children's homes. I could hear Tamla Motown music being played. I had listened to it on my radio sometimes when I was in my room at Auntie Doris's house. I found a corner and sat down. The woman was dashing in and out of the rooms.

"Don't make a mess on the carpet. Don't put your glasses on the floor." She shouted above the music.

"Come and dance." A young man took my handbag off me and put it on the floor. "Who's your father? Which profession is he in?"

I finished dancing and sat down. Soon I was feeling tired and left.

To please Mrs Roth, I rang the number in the Jewish paper looking for people to host house parties. I thought about the size of the house where the party had been held, the people who attended. I didn't think it was a good idea.

I arranged a date for the party. I rang David and asked him if he would come. The night of the party my next door neighbour agreed to have my son stay over with her. I was waiting for the DJ to arrive. David came first. "People aren't going to like this flat. What time's the DJ arriving?"

"I don't know."

"Did you mention for people to bring their own wine with? Have you prepared any food?"

There was a knock on the door. I heard voices David seemed to be taking a long time letting the DJ in. He came back.

"I'm helping him get his records and all his gear. He's blind."

I sat down on the couch. David brought everything in and set it up in the corner. It almost filled the room. The DJ came in wearing dark glasses. He seemed lost and asked to be led to his equipment. Sitting down he put some music on and asked how many people had arrived. I looked at David.

"None yet," I told him.

"Never mind, the night's young."

My heart was pounding at the thought of people arriving. All the feelings of dark self-hatred and loathing filled my head. Someone must have told them the party was being held at Jane Levene's the smelly baked beans flat. I was desperate to eat. I got off the couch to go to the kitchen.

"Has anyone arrived yet?" asked the DJ as he busily felt around his boxes of single records, playing each in turn. "What sort of music do you like?" he asked.

Epilogue

A year later I left Manchester I was 28. I moved in with my husband-to-be. I thought my behaviour was normal, even though I was in a constant state of physical and mental breakdown, my sexual and emotional feelings misplaced and confused, compulsively bingeing and vomiting and frequently running away, in an attempt to find another family in case this one failed. An obsessive 'loop' had developed because of all the years of isolation and lack of stimulation. Every new event and conversation had to be replayed in my mind to the point of mental exhaustion. My husband was deeply concerned. I was admitted to a psychiatric ward. My husband was told that I would never be able to lead an independent life and would always have to remain in institutions. In 1983 I was reluctantly given a place in a psychotherapeutic community. Soon after I was told that I was intelligent and that I could use my intelligence to help myself. I asked how they would 'cure' me. I was told that I had to live with my memories and personality, they couldn't be erased. In psychotherapy I learned about myself, about others and about the real world. In other words I started to develop as a human being with the psychological tools to tentatively navigate my way through life.

When I left the psychotherapeutic community I gradually became aware of how my behaviours had impacted on myself and my family, particularly my son. The only way I could convey to them what had happened to me was to write it down. I have never been able to read a book or novel because it triggers traumatic memories. In order to tell my story I had to re-live my experiences in sequence using my thoughts, feelings and emotions.

I do not use psychiatric terms in my writing because the developing and entrenched behaviours were perfectly normal reactions to abnormal situations.